Advertising Strategy

Second Edition

Brian Sternthal
and
Derek D. Rucker

Kellogg School of Management
Northwestern University

Copley Custom Textbooks

An imprint of XanEdu Publishing, Inc.

ISBN 13: 978-1-58152-764-3
ISBN 10: 1-58152-764-0

Copley Custom Textbooks
An imprint of XanEdu Publishing Inc.
138 Great Road
Acton, Massachusetts 01720
800-562-2147

Please visit our Web site at www.xanedu.com/copley.

Table of Contents

i

About the Authors

Brian Sternthal is the Kraft Professor of Marketing at the Kellogg School of Management, *Northwestern University*. He holds a Ph.D. in Consumer Research from *The Ohio State University*. His research focuses on the factors that influence the persuasive impact of advertising messages. They appear in the *Journal of Consumer Psychology, Journal of Consumer Research*, and *Journal of Marketing Research*. He teaches advertising strategy at the Kellogg School of Management.

Derek D. Rucker is Associate Professor of Marketing at the Kellogg School of Management, *Northwestern University*, where he teaches advertising strategy. He received his Ph.D. in Psychology from *The Ohio State University*. His work focuses on topics such as persuasion, power, and consumer confidence. This work has appeared in the *Journal of Consumer Psychology, Journal of Consumer Research, Journal of Marketing Research*, and *Journal of Personality and Social Psychology*.

Acknowledgements

We would like to thank Erin Rogalski for providing detailed and thoughtful comments on the chapters, Stacy Rucker for proofreading parts of the work, and Sabin Gurung for helping in developing and producing the book. Thanks are also given to Stacy, Charlotte, and Catherine Rucker for their unconditional love and role as muses to the second author. Finally, we also thank our Kellogg students, whose unique insights and experiences have informed the view of advertising strategy presented in this book.

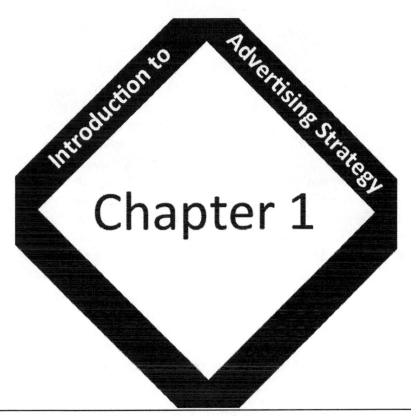

Introduction to Advertising Strategy

Chapter 1

Chapter 1 Objectives

- Define advertising
- Identify the goals that can be achieved by advertising
- Outline the structure of the book: How do you develop effective advertising?

Consider a billboard advertising for *The Economist* business magazine. This billboard was placed in business districts across the US. It features a light bulb on a red background. The light bulb turns on when people pass directly by it. Is this effective advertising? How would you judge its effectiveness and how would you measure it?

This book discusses how to develop persuasive advertising strategies. It is designed not only to answer the question of how to judge and measure advertising effectiveness, though these are central considerations, but also how to develop campaigns that are likely to be effective. We begin by presenting a definition of advertising as a means of identifying the domain of the book. We then describe the steps that are taken to develop and evaluate advertising. This description serves as the basis for the book's structure. In the process, we analyze *The Economist* billboard.

What is Advertising?

The American Marketing Association has defined advertising as any paid form of mass communication by an identified sponsor. This distinguishes advertising from other forms of communication. The fact that it is paid for distinguishes advertising from publicity and word-of-mouth. The fact that it involves mass communication distinguishes it from personal selling. And the fact that it is undertaken by an identified sponsor distinguishes advertising from advocacies by sources that presumably do not benefit directly from the statement of their views.

The mass communication aspect of advertising is implemented through a variety of media. These might include broadcast media such as TV and radio, print media such as newspapers, magazines, and the yellow pages, outdoor media such as billboards and signage, and electronic media such as ads placed on Google and other search sites. But the contemporary conception of advertising media also includes retail establishments such as Benetton and Starbucks, who use their storefronts to inform people of their product offerings, and web sites such as the one for Dove's real beauty campaign (www.campaignforrealbeauty.com/) that elaborate on the brand's values.

What are the Goals of Advertising?

The goal of most advertising is to sustain or increase sales. Advertising is an investment and thus managers are interested in the return on their investment. Although few would dispute the importance of advertising sales goals, communication sub-goals also warrant consideration because their achievement enhances the likelihood of accomplishing sales goals. If advertising is to influence brand sales, people must be motivated to buy the brand. This is achieved by providing information about the brand that attracts consumers' attention. Advertising must also inform consumers that the brand offers a benefit they want and suggest why it does so better than alternatives offerings. Thus, achieving sales goals is based on the achievement of sub-goals including attention to advertising, learning the brand's benefits and motivating the use of this information. Poor performance on these sub-goals provides diagnostic information that can be used to modify the advertising so that it has greater impact on sales.

To illustrate the nature of sub-goals consider again *The Economist* billboard described at the outset of this chapter. Attention to it is likely to be created by the bulb lighting up. Attention is also likely to be attracted by the placement of the billboard in business districts where the information is relevant to passing target consumers. The billboard informs consumers that the bulb will light up when they read *The Economist*. The target readers are smart and witty enough to understand that even they will have thoughts that would not have occurred to them without reading this publication (as depicted by the light bulb being illuminated when they have a close encounter with *The Economist*). Whether this appeal is persuasive enough to prompt reading *The Economist* without the specification of reasons why it will be thought provoking is an empirical question. If it is not, consideration can be given to adding arguments to support the thought-provoking benefit, perhaps using media other than billboards. The use of red prompts an association to *The Economist,* whose masthead is red, and red implies action. Thus, color is likely to provide linkage of the message to the brand and reinforce the action orientation of the publication.

In some situations, the main goal in presenting advertising is not to produce sales. Rather advertising has the function of driving consumers to retail where additional persuasive information is presented to consummate the sale. For example, the goal of car advertising is to create traffic at retail locations where salespeople engage in the personal selling needed to complete the purchase transaction. Here, advertising is part of the sales process, though not the sole or even the most important factor in achieving the sales goal. However, as online car purchasing continues to accelerate, the role of advertising in generating sales might supplant that of personal selling.

Developing Advertising Strategy

Developing advertising is not simply a creative inspiration. It is a systematic process that involves a series of steps, with each step requiring strategic thinking. The process begins with the development of a plan. This plan guides the execution of media and creative strategy. And the adequacy of the plan and its execution are evaluated conceptually and empirically. These steps in the development of advertising strategy are represented in figure 1.1. They represent the structure of this book.

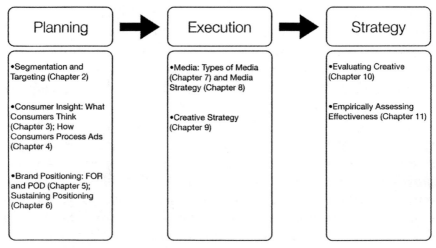

Figure 1.1: The Process of Developing Advertising Strategy

The Planning Process

Advertising begins with planning. Planning for advertising involves engaging in three related types of analysis. One is segmentation and targeting. This involves identifying the groups or segments that have shared goals relevant to the brand and selecting one or more of these segments as the one to target. Segmentation and targeting is examined from an advertising lens in **Chapter 2**. In evaluating the viability of a target, it is important to understand what motivates consumers' consumption of the category and the brand, and how they use this knowledge in making a decision. The development of this consumer insight provides an indication of the brand benefits on which consumers are likely to base their choice. Consumer insight is discussed in **Chapters 3** and **4**. The benefits that are important to consumers on the basis of insight analysis are compared to the benefits that are uniquely offered by a brand. These unique benefits are represented in the brand's position. If a brand is unable to identify unique benefits that are important to consumers, a different target is selected and the process is repeated. **Chapter 5** discusses the development of a brand position and **Chapter 6** examines strategies for sustaining a position. Thus, **Chapters 2-6** are devoted to the planning process. This emphasis reflects the belief that compelling advertising is predicated on a sound plan and that advertising fails because the plan is faulty.

The planning process can be illustrated by considering what a plan might be for *The Economist*. The target and the insight about the target for this magazine can be depicted as follows: highly educated individuals who are interested in international business and political news and views. These individuals are smart, unconventional, and edgy executives or policy-makers who value detailed coverage of global information and appreciate the presentation of a strong point of view on political and business issues. *The Economist's* position is a weekly newspaper (which informs us about the goal) that provides a sophisticated analysis of current issues by taking an editorial stance based on free trade and globalization (which informs us about why *The Economist* is superior in goal achievement).

The Execution Process

Once planning is developed, focus centers on the two activities involved in its execution. One is the development of a media strategy **(Chapter 7)**. This entails making decisions about where and when to advertise so as to maximize target consumers' exposure and attention to the advertising message. The other execution activity pertains to the development of creative strategy **(Chapter 8)**. Here the emphasis is on what to say and how to say it so that the brand position is made operational in a manner that enhances target consumers likelihood of appreciating the brand's benefits and purchasing the brand. *The Economist* uses a unique billboard that has only a light bulb to present the brand's position. The absence of copy beyond the brand name implies that this advertising is self-evident to those who view themselves as the smartest ones in the room. Only they have the wit and intelligence to get what *The Economist* is attempting to convey—that the paper stimulates intelligent thought among those who are intelligent. The choice of a billboard in business districts reflects the effort to reach the target when information about policy and business issues is relevant to them. The use of billboards can be justified because the target is highly knowledgeable about what *The Economist* offers and to provide more information would undermine their special status as sophisticated and knowledgeable individuals.

The Evaluation Process

The evaluation of the advertising that is based on segmentation, targeting and positioning involves two types of analysis. One is to evaluate the creative strategy against criteria that are thought to predict effectiveness. This is the focus of **Chapter 9**, where we examine factors related to Attention, Distinctiveness, Positioning, Linkage, Amplification, and Net equity. The other type of evaluation involves a discussion of the measures and procedures that are useful in empirical tests of advertising effectiveness. These measures and procedures are reviewed in **Chapter 10**.

Summary: The Approach

As our analysis suggests, there are a series of planning and executional steps that are followed in the development of advertising. We shall describe these in detail in this book. Our approach to this discussion is characterized by several features. First, the analysis is theoretically grounded. We develop advertising strategy on the basis of notions of human memory operation in processing and interpreting message information and cues. This theorizing is empirically based, not only on the basis of academic research, but also on the basis of repeated observation of advertising effects in every day settings by advertising strategists. Further, for each of the theoretical ideas developed, we document their value in terms of current advertising practice.

Because our approach to advertising strategy is theoretical, it is also distinguished by the view that advertising operates in an interactive environment. It is common practice in advertising to develop main effect ideas, that is, something is good or bad: humor is more persuasive than threat, three exposures are sufficient for persuasion, comparison advertising is advertising for the competitor. Our approach is interactive. The question we pose is not whether a strategy is effective or not, but under what consumer, competitive and environmental conditions will it be effective. This implies that rather than rules for advertising strategy, we develop an assessment of why a strategy works (i.e., theoretical analysis), which will be informative about when it will work. In our discussions of planning and execution, a consideration of the interactive advertising environment is facilitated by developing a series of ordered questions that should be addressed in the pursuit of effective advertising strategy, and we use current knowledge to help answer these questions.

Finally, our approach is based on the belief that advertising is an empirical business. Even sound strategies can yield poor performance because of a myriad of unanticipated factors including consumer reactions, competitor strategies, and environmental occurrences. The hallmark of successful management of the advertising function is not the development of error-free strategy, but rather the speed and thoughtfulness with which strategists respond to the outcomes observed in the marketplace. Thus, we shall place a premium on data as a basis for strategy.

Chapter 2 Objectives

- Development of effective advertising segmentation strategies to grow a brand
- Exploration of the rationales behind various targeting strategies
- Advertising to current users: Brand users and competitors' users
- Strategies for advertising to non-users
  - o Point of entry
  - o Category build
- Considerations for advertising to multiple segments simultaneously
- Segmentation on the basis of buying center function

A survey of dog owners' motivations and behavior suggests that they can be classified into three categories: Social Dog Lovers, Functional dog owners and Price Seekers (see figure 2.1).

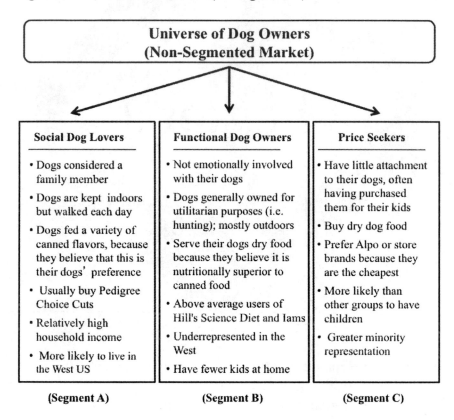

Figure 2.1: Classification of Dog Owners

   This analysis depicts the process by which segmentation and targeting strategies for advertising are developed. Segmentation is the process of dividing customers into groups with similar characteristics. Initially segments are identified on the basis of insights regarding some distinction among them and some commonalities within each segment. As seen in the dog owner example, each segment is identified on the basis of certain common consumer characteristics, while ignoring the nonessential differences. This process of grouping consumers according to their unique needs or behaviors enables a company to design products that satisfy these needs in a more effective way than through a "one size fits all" approach. Once segments are established, a brand selects one or more segments for which it can deliver, through advertising, the segment's desired benefit better than competitors.

In this chapter, we discuss how to sustain and grow brand performance by developing effective segmentation and targeting strategies. A starting point involves the identification of current users and those most likely to be brand users on the basis of insights about their motivations for consumption. Then we assess the wisdom of targeting competitors' users. We also discuss strategies for brand growth that involve attracting nonusers of the category. These include point-of-entry and category build strategies. Finally, we suggest decision criteria to determine whether or not to advertise to two segments simultaneously.

Usage-Based Segmentation and Targeting

Most brands pursue a segmentation strategy where consumers' goals can be particularly well satisfied by a brand's offering. However, segmentation is not the place to start the targeting analysis. Initially an effort is made to target all consumers, that is, no segmentation. When it becomes evident that there are segments that are not attractive to a brand, as is commonly the case, targeting specific segments becomes appropriate.

Segmentation is often discussed in terms of demographics and psychographics. Although these bases are important when trying to make segmentation decisions operational, the most frequently used basis for designing segmentation strategy is usage. Within usage four distinct segments exist: (i) current users of the brand, (ii) competitors' users, (iii) point of entry, and (iv) category build. As the targeting usage model depicted in the figure 2.2 suggests, a starting point for segmentation analysis involves an assessment of category users including brand and competitors' users because these consumers are familiar with the category.

Once there is saturation of the current user target, or it is not viable to attract competitors' users, attention turns to converting nonusers of the category to users of the brand. This can be achieved by

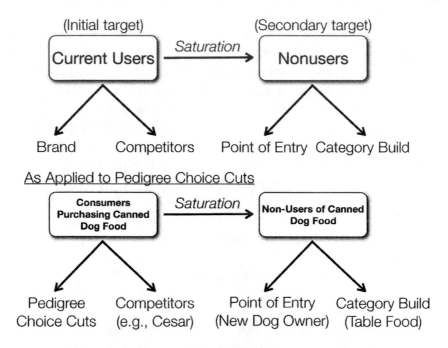

Figure 2.2: Targeting Strategies (top panel) and Application to Pedigree (bottom panel)

targeting point-of-entry, which refers to those who have not yet entered the category but are about to do so. For example, consumers who purchased their first dog would be point-of-entry consumers for dog food. Nonusers of the category can also be targeted using a category build strategy. This entails attracting consumers who achieve the goal accomplished by a brand's category in some other way. In the case of dog food, category build might involve targeting consumers who feed their dogs table food. We shall elaborate on when each of these targeting strategies warrants consideration.

Targeting Brand Users

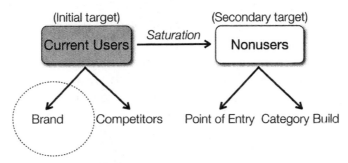

For established brands, the attractiveness of a target composed of current brand users and especially the heavy users of the brand is assessed first when developing a targeting strategy. For most brands, 80% of the consumption is done by 20% of the users. For example, a heavy user of Campbell's soup purchases more than 300 cans a year, suggesting a consumption rate of close to a can a day!

The way people process information and make decisions provides a rationale for why current users are considered first when developing a targeting strategy. As shown in figure 2.3, new information such as that in an advertisement is initially represented in a temporary store that we shall refer to as the short-term memory (**#1** in the diagram). Short-term memory is active memory. It represents what you are thinking at the moment. And what you are thinking at the moment can be a combination of new information and information you had acquired previously, which is represented in long-term memory, the repository of all knowledge (**#2**). Short-term memory is only capable of holding a limited amount of information and for only a short period of time. As a consequence, for new information to be accessible in the future, it must be stored in long-term memory. Important information is transferred from short-term to long-term memory by a process of amplification that associates new and prior knowledge (**#3**).

The information represented in long-term memory is organized so as to facilitate its later location and retrieval. One way information in long-term memory is organized is in terms of meaning. Along these lines, it is thought that meaning of a brand derives, in part, from its association with a category as shown in the diagram.

For example, telling people a brand is a computer informs them about the goal that can be achieved by using it.

Typically not all information represented in long-term memory that might be relevant to making a decision is retrieved into the short-term store and used to make a decision. This is because long-term memory is a repository of all knowledge, whereas short-term memory is limited in capacity. The information that is most accessible is likely to be retrieved from long-term memory, represented in short-term memory, and used to make a judgment or choice (**#4**).

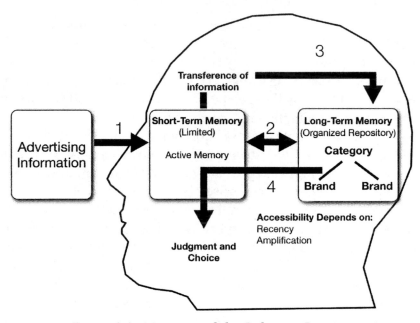

Figure 2.3: Memory and the Judgment Process

Information is most accessible when it has been processed recently (*Recency*) and when it has been accessed or thought about extensively in association with other thoughts (*Amplification*). Furthermore, even if information in long-term memory is accessible, it might not be activated because the effort required for such activation is not worth the potential gain from its activation. Message recipients usually reserve the allocation of their scarce cognitive resources for the processing of information that presents news. Thus, for retrieval to take place information must be both accessible and worth the cognitive effort to extract.

To illustrate this judgment process, consider how consumers might respond to a new advertising message for Tropicana orange juice, which states that the beverage has a superior taste because it is fresh and not from concentrate. A recipient of this message might represent it more or less accurately in short-term memory (See **#1** in figure 2.4). In turn, this representation might activate the retrieval of the message recipient's knowledge relevant to Tropicana from long-term memory. For example, the message recipient might recall a prior ad that mentioned Tropicana is made within 24 hours of picking the oranges (**#2**). This retrieved reason to believe in Tropicana's quality might then be associated in short term memory with the fact that it is not from concentrate, resulting in the storage of these two reasons to believe Tropicana's quality in long-term memory (i.e., amplification **#3**). The availability of multiple associations to a benefit increases the likelihood that this information will be accessible to evaluate alternative brands of orange juice and make a choice among them (**#4**).

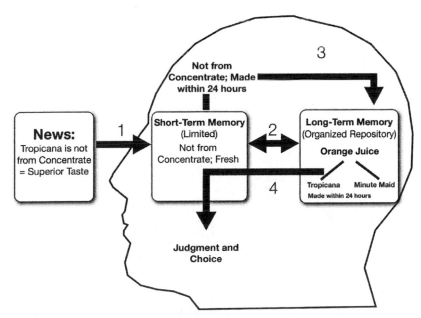

Figure 2.4: Example of Model of Human Memory
Applied to Tropicana Advertising

This view of the judgment process implies that *much of the persuasion in response to advertising and other marketing instruments is self-persuasion.* Advertising prompts people to activate and use their own ad-related knowledge as a basis for brand judgments. This depiction suggests that current users should be the center of focus because they are most likely to activate a repertoire of favorable brand associations in response to an advertising message and thus have a high probability of purchasing the brand. Stated another way, a current user target is easiest to persuade because their accepted beliefs are consistent with what the brand offers. Following this approach, efforts to increase brand consumption are achieved by prompting greater use by current users and by attracting more people with the same profile as current users.

As important as current heavy users of a brand are to a franchise, it is remarkable how frequently firms walk away from this equity. Sometimes this is done in the name of ensuring the modernity of the brand. General Foods' Sugar Crisp cereal had an impressive 2% share during a $7 billion cereal business. However, when General Mills led the trend toward non-sugared sweet cereals with their introduction of Honey Nut Cheerios, General Foods changed Sugar Crisp to Golden Crisp, dropped the highly recognized and liked Sugar Bear mascot, and succeeded in losing more than half of the brand's franchise (i.e., $70 million dollars in annual revenue).

Targeting Competitor's Users

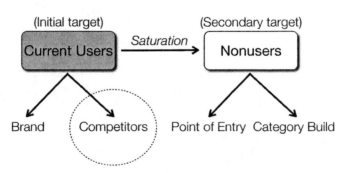

Once demand among current users of a brand is saturated, attention often turns to attracting competitors' users of the brand. The advantage with competitors' users is that they are already convinced about the virtue of the category. The disadvantage is that their preference for their current brand needs to be overcome. An assessment of this opportunity begins with a determination of the size of the opportunity. Competitors who attract heavy users of the category are considered first. An assessment is made of whether a brand is positioned in a manner that can attract competitors' users. For example does a brand have a superior benefit in relation to its competition?

Even if this targeting strategy is promising, before proceeding an evaluation is needed to determine competitors' ability and motivation to mount a defense against an attack. Does the competitor have the financial resources to combat an attack on its brand's users? If so, does the competitor have the motivation to defend the brand? A brand defense is usually most vigorous when the brand is central to the competitor's portfolio. For example, Gillette is more likely to defend strongly against an attack on its target in the blade and shaving cream categories than in the body wash category. If the competition lacks a means of responding this can be a viable target.

The risk in targeting competition's customers is that it incites a competitive battle with each company offering incentives to switch consumers to its brand. Escalating demands to attract customers can ultimately damage the entire category. When strong retribution is expected, a brand might consider somewhat less attractive growth opportunities such as consumers attracted by smaller competitors that are less capable of a defense against attack, or the introduction of strategies to attract category nonusers. However, if a company does decide to go head-to-head in a battle for consumers, it would utilize advertising messages to highlight unique characteristics and features about the product. A famous example of this strategy is the Pepsi Challenge, where Pepsi showed people preferring that brand over Coke in a blind taste test. Pepsi made significant inroads on Coke by pursuing this strategy.

Category Nonusers

Two types of nonusers warrant evaluation in an effort to achieve brand growth. One segment is composed of those who are actively considering the entry into the category, that is, point-of-entry consumers. The other nonuser segment is composed of individuals who do not plan to use the category in which your brand holds membership because the benefit provided by this category is being met through another means. Here, the task is to build the category in which the brand is a member by convincing people that your category provides a better means of achieving some desired outcome than the category currently being used by consumers.

Point of Entry

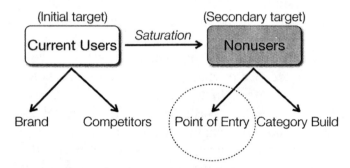

To illustrate point-of-entry, consider the tale of Carie Slaughter who arrives at Northwestern to begin her college education on September 21st. When she checks into her dorm, she receives a coupon valued at $5.00 on any purchase of $20 or more at the CVS pharmacy; and within a few days a credit card application arrives in the mail from Chase Bank. Carie also sees an ad for Lakeshore Cleaners in the *Daily Northwestern.* Later she receives an email for a half price pizza at Giordano's. All of these brands recognize that consumers who are starting college are *active* in changing their status from non-category users to category users and thus are decisional about which brand to purchase. We refer to this target as point-of-entry. The idea underlying a point-of-entry strategy is a) to identify who will be entering the category and b) to use advertising to direct these consumers to purchase the firm's brand. Point-of-entry is analogous to a first-mover strategy, but here the consumer is new to the category rather than the product being new to the consumer.

Point-of-entry targeting is a particularly attractive strategy when two conditions exist: Low brand penetration and high loyalty. Brand penetration refers to the percent of category users that have used the brand during a specific time period (usually one year, though it varies with repeat purchase frequency). For example, Gain detergent has about 10% annual penetration, which means that of every 10 consumers who used detergent in a year, one purchased Gain at least once. This penetration is low compared to Tide, which has about 90% penetration. Penetration might be low because a brand has only a niche target and thus there are many nonusers of the brand. Penetration can also be low because consumers who once used the brand have abandoned it as a result of deterioration in the brand's quality or reputation. And penetration can be low because consumers are loyal to a rival brand. When penetration is low, focusing on building the number of people who try the brand can grow a brand's franchise. However, if point-of-entry is to be a viable strategy, it is also important to gain loyalty among those who are attracted to the brand. That is, advertising can funnel non-users towards a brand, but there must be other mechanisms in place to ensure the loyalty of those who try the brand.

The most common loyalty efforts involve promotions such as frequent buyer cards and "buy two, get one free deals." For example, airline frequent flyer programs and credit card reward programs are loyalty devices. Advertising that reminds customers of its benefits or introduces new benefits can also be an effective means of sustaining loyalty. Gaining loyalty is particularly important because a point-of-entry strategy often involves a relatively narrow target. Along these lines, the heavy drinker of beer is 21-34 year old, but the point-of-entry is typically much narrower, say 21-28 or 21-24.

Another approach to ensuring that a point-of-entry strategy targets a substantial number of new users is to construe it to include users of the category who were not previously decisional about the brand. Students who start college have used a variety of grooming products when living at home, but they might not have been decisional about the brand of soap, shampoo, toothpaste or detergent that they used. They used whatever was in the house. These individuals will be active in selecting a brand and thus can be treated as point-of-entry consumers. Similarly, parents, might be point-of-entry for the first time with respect to diapers with their first child or because they revisit what brands to use when their second child arrives.

Category Build

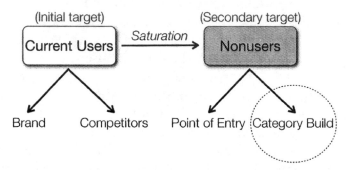

Like point-of-entry, a category build strategy is focused on non-users. However, category build is directed toward those who are *passive*; they have no intention of using the category in which the brand holds membership to achieve a particular goal. For example, one might promote the use of electronic organizers to those who use a conventional appointment book. Category build is an appropriate strategy when a) there is a lack of saturation of the category and b) the firm has a means of directing the demand generated for the category to its brand.

The lack of category saturation that prompts consideration of a category build emerges in a variety of circumstances. It can occur when a category is new, as was the case with yogurt in the 1980s, sports utility vehicles in the mid-1990s and MP3 players and energy drinks more recently. A lack of saturation can also occur in a mature category that has lost its consumer base. For example, in 1990, per capita consumption of coffee was about 65% of the level it had enjoyed in 1960, largely because the 90s generation of young people drank far less coffee than its earlier counterpart. Or, the lack of saturation might be attributable to consumers' failure to recognize the problem for which the category is a remedy. This situation arises frequently in the pharmaceutical arena where consumers are unaware of their depression, low thyroid condition, and the like, and thus do not prompt their physicians to prescribe the ethical products available to remedy these conditions. Finally, categories with seasonal skews in sales, such as BBQ sauce may be unsaturated contra-seasonally. A majority of the BBQ sauce in the U.S. is sold for Memorial Day, July 4th and Labor Day holidays. Advertising at other times of the year thus might serve to stimulate category use during non-holiday periods.

There are a variety of devices that are used to direct the demand generated by a category build to a firm's brand. Most frequently, the assumption is that brands will attract category sales in proportion to their share of market. Thus, it is typical for market leaders to engage in category build. However, leadership is but one means of directing category demand to a specific brand. In the absence of market leadership, firms with stronger sales forces than the competition might use advertising to build the category and employ their sales force to direct this demand to the firm's brand.

A major impediment to introducing a category build strategy is the lack of certitude about whether demand in a category is saturated or not. Electric razors are purchased by about 40% of the U.S. population. Is this category saturated or not? Two-thirds of the estimated million people who suffer from depression use anti-depressant medication such as Prozac. Is this category saturated, or is there an opportunity to build the category? Assessing the level of saturation is an issue that benefits from research that illuminates the factors responsible for people's failure to use a category. The prospects for a successful category build are far greater if research suggests the category growth is constrained by a lack of category awareness than if category growth is constrained due to a negative disposition toward the category. Consumers who have once used a category and no longer do so are typically poor prospects for a category build, unless there is category news that has emerged since they used the product. Consumers who were once consumers of milk, peanut butter, soft drinks, and the like and who have stopped using these categories as they grew older are typically poor candidates for category build strategies in the absence of significant category news. In addition, as we discuss in a later section of this chapter, insight about the extent of saturation and the appropriateness of a category build may be inferred by an assessment of brand performance in relation to category performance.

Targeting Multiple Segments Simultaneously

Our analysis of user and nonuser targets raises the possibility of targeting multiple segments simultaneously. When considering multiple segments, we recommend organizing them on the basis of their importance to the brand. Specifically, one can consider targeting priorities with respect to a "bulls-eye" depicted in the following diagram (figure 2.5). At the center of the bulls-eye is the "own" target. This target is most critical to the health of a brand. An "attract" target is one that helps to sustain the brand over time. Finally, an "accept" target is composed of people who it is important not to alienate. To illustrate, for Harley-Davidson, the own target is composed of burly blue collar guys who sport tattoos and would be likely to beat the crap out of you if they looked at you. This target is critical because it is a magnet for the other targets. The "attract" target is composed of Gen Y males (born after 1982) who are point-of-entry consumers and are likely to buy a brand with a more contemporary image such as Suzuki, Honda, Yamaha, or Kawasaki than a Harley. This target is important because it represents the next generation of Harley owners. Finally, Harley needs to accept the spouses of potential riders so that they do not block purchasing of the product.

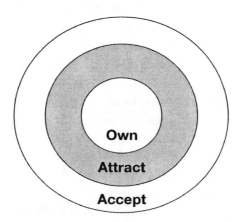

Figure 2.5: The Targeting Bulls-eye

How do brands that have the advertising budget to target multiple segments such as Harley decide whether or not it is prudent to do so? A determination of whether multiple segments are viable or whether a single target should be selected can be addressed by answering a series of questions illustrated in Figure 2.6.

First, a brand should ask whether there is saturation among its current users (**#1**). As noted earlier, if usage is not saturated among current users, it is often significantly easier to encourage these users to consume more since they are already likely to accept the brand's positioning. If growth is not possible among current users, a brand should next ask itself whether current users are protected (**#2**). If current users are not protected and can be stolen the value of new users must be weighed against the potential loss of current users. If the value of new users does not exceed the anticipated loss of current users then this suggest retaining current users. This may also suggest that marketing can only maintain the status quo and that growth must be sought elsewhere. If currents use are protected, or the value of new users is deemed worth the potential risk, the next question that should be asked is whether current users might be alienated from the proposed advertising strategy and/or execution (**#3**). If the answer is no, the potential risk and degree of alienation among current users must be considered. If users are safe from alienation (e.g,. content will not alienate, or media used to selectively target new users) or the degree of risk is viewed as acceptable, the brand is in position to target the new segment.

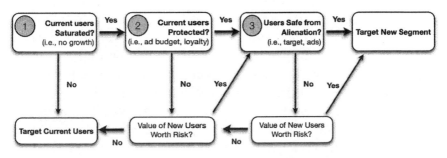

Figure 2.6: Targeting Multiple Users

A recent campaign for Red Bull illustrates the use of these criteria. Red Bull is an energy drink that is targeted primarily at Gen Y males—those between 18-30. This is Red Bull's "own" target. Red Bull is consumed primarily as a social drink. It is often combined with vodka to provide a sensation of being speeded up and slowed down at the same time. Brand promotion initially involved sponsorship of extreme sports events (e.g., BMX biking, kite-boarding, skydiving) with trendsetters in the youth culture, giving Red Bull its street credibility. As brand demand grew, the "Red Bull gives you wiiings" campaign was introduced. One television execution showed a cartoon of people using the product being able to fly and engage in crude retributive behavior against birds. Although Red Bull's share of the energy drink market was 43%, its rate of growth in sales was declining. And, strong competition was anticipated from Monster and Rockstar.

To sustain its growth, Red Bull considered expanding its targeting efforts. One target that appeared attractive was golfers. It was found that a substantial numbers of golfers used Red Bull to sustain their energy through 18 holes. Consideration was given to targeting these individuals using a celebrity golfer such as Jack Nicklaus and at the same time continuing the wiiings campaign to the Gen Y own target.

To assess the opportunity for Red Bull presented by golfers, consider the criteria we developed. Red Bull had a need to grow the user base. With the entry of competitors and slowing growth in consumption among current users (i.e., a sign of saturation), it was judicious to consider a new target. As the leading brand, Red Bull had the resources both to protect current users and to target golfers. At issue was whether efforts to attract might alienate current users. Golfers' average age is 50. Even though older adults aspired to be more youthful, advertising to golfers would require a different type of campaign than that used to attract Gen Y. And abandoning current users in favor of older adults did not appear to be viable because most of the current demand for Red Bull, which was substantial, was sourced from current Gen Y users. Therefore, for new users to be viable the brand had to find a way to limit exposure of their new targeting efforts to Gen Y users.

Fortunately, this issue seemed easy to address by using media such as *Golf Magazine* and golfing tournaments to advertise Red Bull, which were not read by Gen Y. Therefore, although there was the possibility that seeing older individuals consuming Red Bull might alienate the current user, by using different media forms, and a common voice of sports energy on their website, the brand attempted to navigate both groups.

The strategy pursued by most brands is to focus on a single target. To ensure that the brand captures the own target, advertising sometimes alienates nonusers. The idea is to have users feel that the brand is just for them. Red Bull's depiction of crude behaviors in advertising attracts Gen Y, in part by presenting images that are viewed by the target as alienating nonusers.

The Buying Center

To this point, our analysis of segmentation and targeting for advertising has been based on usage. Segmentation can also be based on the functions an individual performs in the buying center. These include: influencer, decider, purchaser, and user. In business-to-business settings, engineers serve as influencers, VPs of marketing or finance as deciders, purchasing agents are the purchasers, and operatives are the users. In some consumer settings, the buying center might include the parents as deciders and purchasing agents, and kids as influencers and users.

Segmentation on the basis of the role played in the buying center is appropriate when different instruments are needed to attract different segments. Engineers might want advertising that focuses on product specs, whereas purchasing agents might be most interested in product price. Similarly, for a consumer food product, kid users might be interested in advertising that featured the product's taste, whereas the parents might be more responsive to information about the nutritional quality of the product. Alternatively, the adult purchaser might be targeted as the purchaser and persuaded to purchase the product for their children on the basis of a kid benefit such as taste.

Another way to conceptualize the buying center is to view both the distribution channel and ultimate consumers as its members. In developing advertising messages to consumers, efforts are also made to energize the channel. For example, manufacturers in bottling businesses such as soft drinks and beer recognize that bottlers are instrumental in determining brand sales. They use consumer advertising as one of the devices to motivate the bottlers by showing how strong the brand is and how easily it will sell. Vehicles such as the Superbowl are used by franchisers to enhance good feelings that store operators as well as consumers have toward the brand. By advertising *to* the channel as well as *through* the channel, the goal is to reinforce the same brand position to both resellers and consumers.

Bases for Segmentation

We have suggested that segmentation and targeting strategy are based on usage and an individual's role in the buying center. Once a target is selected, it requires a demographic, psychographic or geographic description if media vehicles such as radio, TV or the internet are to be found to reach the target with advertising. Whether the target should be described in terms of demographics or psychographics is subject to debate. Should the target for dog food be described in terms of age and income, or in terms of whether they are Social Dog Lovers or Functional owners?

A common observation is that users and nonusers have the same demographics in many product categories. This has prompted greater reliance on psychographic bases for segmentation, which do a better job of discriminating between users and nonusers. The problem with this approach is that media and vehicles where these people might be reached are not always clear. For example, it seems relatively easy to find online vehicles to reach the Functional dog owner (e.g., websites related to hunting); but it is less obvious what vehicles you might employ to advertise to Price Seekers. When psychographic targeting is difficult to execute, demographics are used because surveys provide a demographic profile of those exposed to different advertising vehicles. Even in these instances, the psychographic analysis is useful in designing a brand's position and in developing the creative execution.

Segmentation and targeting can also be based on geography. When a firm has distribution in multiple areas of the country, it can create a brand development index (BDI). This is computed by dividing the per capita sales for the brand in a particular region by the per capita sales for the brand in the country as a whole and multiplying by 100. For example, if Tide's per capita sales in Chicago are say $250 per year, whereas in the country as a whole they are $125 per year, the BDI for Chicago is 200 (250/125x100). An index of 200 does not necessarily mean that the brand is strong in Chicago. This would depend on the brand's market share. What a BDI of 200 indicates is that Chicago per capita sales of the brand are twice that of the country for a given population. In this way, regions can be divided into low and high BDI areas.

A similar analysis can be done at the category level to compute a category development index (CDI). This entails a consideration of the per capita sales of the category in a region in relation to the per capita sales of the category for the entire country. For example, if the per capita sales of laundry detergent in Chicago were $2500 and the sales of laundry detergent across the country was $1000, this would lead to a CDI of 250 (2500/1000x100), which would suggest two and a half times the per capita consumption of the category in Chicago compared to the national average. This computation allows the determination of high and low category development or CDI areas.

The product of this analysis is a fourfold classification that can serve as a useful basis for designing targeting strategy that reflects competitors' strengths and weaknesses (figure 2.7). For areas where both the category and the brand exhibit high indices, the first course of action is typically to sustain demand. Market saturation might have set in and investment spending might not be warranted. However, it is possible that a brand with a high BDI can make inroads in a high CDI area if the brand's market share is relatively low. In contrast, a low CDI and high BDI suggest an opportunity to build the category. Caution is necessary here to ensure that a) the market is not saturated and b) category leadership or some other means is available of directing the demand created for the category to the brand. In situations where there is high CDI but low BDI, there might be an opportunity to grow the brand. Here, the market might be penetrated if a brand has a point of difference in relation to competitors on dimensions important to consumers. A point-of-entry strategy might be warranted if the low brand penetration is accompanied by strategies to stimulate brand loyalty. Finally, when both CDI and BDI are low, it might be possible to build the category, though here the judicious approach might be not to support the brand.

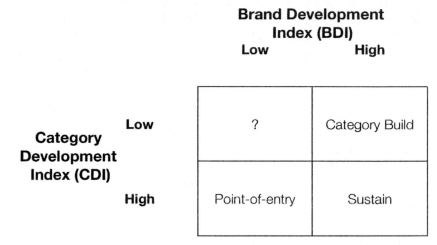

Figure 2.7: Implications of Brand Development Index for Targeting

It is important to recognize that the foregoing framework is useful in identifying potential opportunities. Whether a brand can take advantage of the opportunity requires additional consider-ations related to consumers and competitors. For example, Bulls-eye barbeque (BBQ) sauce has low BDI in the Southwest, which is a high CDI region for BBQ sauce. Market penetration in this area seems attractive, except that KC Masterpiece is the major brand in this region and consumers in this region prefer KC's Memphis-style flavor to that of Bulls-eye. In addition, KC Masterpiece would respond strongly to Bulls-eye's attempt to steal share, which given the relative strength of the brands would make this strategy un-attractive. Alternatively, Bulls-eye might attempt to build the category in the central region of the country where its BDI is high and the CDI is low. This opportunity would seem particularly attractive if Bulls-eye also had the largest market share in this region.

Although a BDI/CDI analysis is often illuminating about the type of opportunity that exists in different locales, it typically has limited applicability when segmentation and targeting involve advertising. This is because firms typically do not segment on the basis of geography such that different campaigns are run in different parts of the country. This is not because this segmentation is not effective; rather it is because it is viewed as too costly. For example, Network TV costs about the same as that required to cover half the country with segmented region-by-region advertising. The cost of additional creative for different regions exacerbates the problem. Similarly, developing custom websites can quickly add up, and funneling different consumers can be a daunting task. Thus, unless there is evidence that geographic segmentation will be highly effective, its lack of efficiency limits its use in most cases. Instead, advertising covers the entire market, and brands heavy up the expenditure against current users and nonuser opportunities.

Summary of Segmentation and Targeting Strategy

Segmentation and targeting strategy is depicted in the diagram below. It begins with a consideration of current users of the brand because they are likely to be favorably disposed to both the category and the brand and thus easiest to persuade. Growth can be achieved by persuading current brand users to consume more. Alternately, competitors' users might be targeted if the brand has a strong point of difference and has the financial resources to compete.

Once the consumption by these targets is saturated, focus centers on nonusers. Point-of-entry is a viable target when brand penetration is low and brand loyalty is high. It entails guiding those who are actively becoming users of the category to become users of the brand. Category build is viable when the category is unsaturated and the brand has category leadership or has some other means of converting category demand into demand for the brand. Category build entails persuading people that the category in which a brand has membership is a better means of achieving some goal than by using an alternative category. Finally, whether multiple targets are sought or not depends on need, budget, protection, conflict, and opportunity as figure 2.8 indicates.

In some contexts, the target's function in the buying center rather than usage might be used as the basis for segmentation. The buying center may be composed of individuals with different goals—influencing, deciding, purchasing, and using. Alternatively the buying center might be composed of the distribution channel and consumers. When people performing different functions have different goals, a consideration is given to the function served in the buying center as a basis for segmentation.

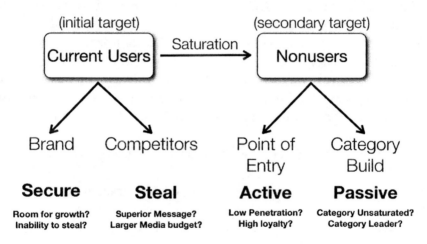

Figure 2.8: Usage Based Segmentation and Targeting Summary

Chapter Exercises

- Choose a current advertising campaign. Can you identify the target from a usage, demographic and psychographic perspective? Is the company pursuing an appropriate target? Why or Why not?

- Develop a segmentation and targeting analysis for iPhone. Identify the various segments that might be targeted and provide a rationale for the one that would be targeted first.

- You are the brand manager for an ice cream chain and are planning to start some out-of-home advertising in the form of store competitions as well as billboards. You have stores in five different markets and have obtained information about your brand as well as the category (see table below). Based on the information presented below, how would you spend your advertising dollars? Would you adopt a similar spend in all five cities, or would you favor some cities over others? Finally, do you have reason to suspect your opportunity for growth varies as a function of the city?

	CDI	BDI	SIZE
City 1	150	100	500,000
City 2	100	150	300,000
City 3	100	100	300,000
City 4	200	50	2,000,000
City 5	50	200	120,000

Recommended Reading

Howes, Mary B. (2007), *Human Memory, Structure and Images*, Sage Publications, Thousand Oaks, CA.

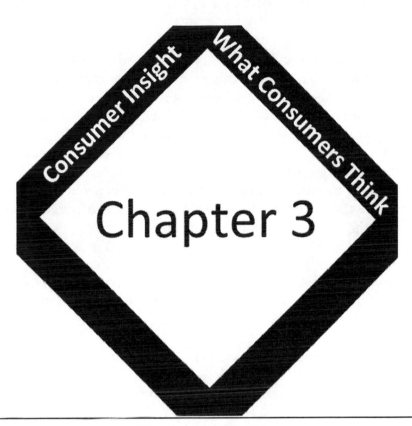

Consumer Insight   What Consumers Think

Chapter 3

Chapter 3 Objectives

- Category and brand beliefs
- Factors influencing beliefs
    - Consumer Goals
    - Stage in the life cycle
    - Generational effects
    - Individual differences:
      Age, social class, gender

Knowledge of what consumers think about a brand and the category in which it holds membership is fundamental to developing effective advertising strategy. As we illustrated with the segmentation analysis of dog owners in **Chapter 2**, such consumer insight highlights consumers' goals, which are assessed in relation to a brand's position to determine the viability of attracting specific segments. Insight about what consumers think is assessed in a variety of ways. As a starting point, we examine the value of insight about consumers' beliefs pertaining to the brand and the category in which it holds membership in designing advertising strategy. Then, the value of insights provided by beliefs that are related to a consumers' stage in the lifecycle and the generation in which they grew up are assessed. Finally, we examine the role of insights derived from individual differences in consumers' age, social class, and gender in articulating a brand's position and the creative execution.

Usage-Based Segmentation and Targeting

How do you determine whether a brand is likely to be attractive to a specific target? A starting point to address this question typically involves an assessment of consumers' beliefs about both the category and one's brand. One type of belief pertains to functional benefits of the category and brand. For example, two widely accepted consumer beliefs are that regular ready-to-eat cereal is nutritious, and that Cheerios is among the most nutritious brands of ready-to-eat cereal. In addition, many consumers hold the (false) belief that honey is more nutritional than sugar. General Mills adapted to these beliefs by developing Honey Nut Cheerios, which was positioned not only as being nutritious, but also as tasting better than other regular cereals because it used honey (rather than sugar) as the sweetening agent. Honey Nut Cheerios quickly became a leading brand of ready-to-eat cereal. This success was based on insight about consumers' category and brand beliefs.

Another type of belief relates to the motivation or symbolism that using a category and brand reflects or provides. The motivation for eating ready-to-eat cereal might be to enhance one's sense of well being; the motivation for purchasing a sports car such as a Porsche might be to feel empowered. The motivation for baking a cake might be to exhibit affection for one's family. This latter insight was the basis for the Pillsbury baked goods campaign slogan, "nothing says lovin' as something from the oven." Advertising that recognizes the symbolism of a brand or category and supports consumers' motivations for using them enhances the impact of the brand message.

Although the strategy of first resort is to position a brand so as to embrace or at least accommodate consumers' current beliefs, there are situations where it is necessary to change category and brand beliefs. This occurs when a defining characteristic of the category is viewed negatively. The majority of consumers believe that electric razors do not give as close a shave as blade razors, that milk has high fat content and that frozen pizza does not taste very good. Advertising for these categories must necessarily confront accepted consumer beliefs. In addition, brands can be associated with beliefs to which it cannot adapt. Kraft branded their premium brands such as Philadelphia Cream Cheese under a separate name rather than as a member of the Kraft family, because consumers believe that Kraft's quality is good but not premium.

Factors Influencing Consumers' Beliefs

Consumers' beliefs about product categories and brands, and their motivations for using them are influenced by a variety of factors. These include their personal goals, stage in the lifecycle, generation, and individual differences in age, social class, and gender. These factors prompt the activation of a lens that influences the judgments consumers make. Knowledge of these factors allows anticipation of whether or not and how a consumer segment will be attracted to a brand.

Consumer Goals

One way to develop an understanding of consumers' goals is to conduct a psychographic analysis. This approach focuses on lifestyle rather than demographic information as a basis for describing segments and entails asking questions about activities, interests and opinions. In some instances, psychographic measures are customized for the brand of interest. In other situations, data collected by commercial services are used. To illustrate the nature of this segmentation analysis, consider the psychographic approach developed by SRI. Their psychographic instrument, VALS (Values and Lifestyle Program), is a self-administered questionnaire. It is comprised of questions pertaining to your attitudes and opinions on topics such as travel, fashion and shopping. You can take this survey at http://www.sric-bi.com (vals survey), and examine the predictions made about your behavior. SRI uses this questionnaire in conjunction with proprietary and nonproprietary databases on current consumer demographics, psychographics, and spending patterns to help their clients develop segmentation, targeting and positioning strategies.

One question that often arises with regard to VALS and other psychometric measures is whether these measures can be used in lieu of demographic information to identify targets. As noted in **Chapter 2**, most psychographic measures are not substitutes for demographic data because the psychographic measures are not linked to media consumption habits (VALS and PRIZM are exceptions). Thus, it is usually not possible to link a target to the media it reads and watches. Further, none of the psychographic services identify individuals in a manner that allows the recruitment of similar research participants if they are needed for further research. Some psychographic services address this problem by correlating the psychographic measures with demographic ones and then using the demographic profile to recruit research respondents. But this solution underscores the fact that psychographic measures are best viewed as a supplement that enriches the description of the target rather than as a replacement for target demographics.

A tool that is growing in usage is segmentation based on geodemographic data. The insight behind the geodemographic methodology is that people who live in the same neighborhood are more likely to have similar characteristics than people chosen at random. Based on this concept, various tools categorize neighborhoods based on the populations which they contain. Two neighborhoods can be placed in the same category even though they are geographically dispersed.

One popular geodemographic segmentation device that is available in the United States is PRIZM (Potential Rating Index by Zip Market). PRIZM combines socio-economic data (i.e. household income, home value, age) with lifestyle attributes (i.e. new car purchases, vacation destinations, favorite brands) to classify every U.S. zip code into 66 distinct categories. Some example customer segments include the "Heartlanders," a segment that typically includes middle-aged couples with working-class jobs pursuing a rustic life and living in sturdy, unprctentious homes. The segment's prime leisure activities include hunting, fishing, camping and boating. The "Young Influentials" category includes the emerging urban yuppie class while the "Park Bench Seniors" segment represents single retirees living quiet, low-key lifestyles in ethnically diverse neighborhoods:
www.tetrad.com/pub/documents/pnesegments.pdf.

PRIZM has recently teamed up with comScore, a marketing research firm specializing in digital marketing intelligence, to measure and report the online behavior of internet users across 66 PRIZM clusters for an even more robust segment analysis (for more details consult:
www.comscore.com/Products_Services/Product_Index/Segmentation_Studies/Segment_Metrix_for_PRIZM. A similar concept has been developed by Global MOSAIC that categorizes neighborhoods, but rather than focusing on the groups within a single country, collects data from over 16 countries and 280 million households. Global Mosaic has organized the world's residential neighborhoods into 10 segments which include such groups as the "Sophisticated Singles," "Metropolitan Strugglers," and "Comfortable Retirement." Information about Global Mosaic is found at:
www.appliedgeographic.com/Mosaic Global E-Handbook.pdf.

As we noted, the primary analysis of consumer segments and targets is typically performed using demographic data. Psychographic data supplements demographic data to offer insight about consumers' goals and dispositions, which is particularly useful in presenting a brand's position and in the execution of creative strategy. However, there are occasions when knowing the psychographic profile of the customer allows for an educated guess about the media that would be appropriate to reach them. Online services track the internet locations that have been visited by consumers and on this basis inferences about consumers' motivations and goals can be made. Brands contract with websites such as Google Search, so that when consumers whose goals match that of a brand click on that website, an ad for the brand appears on that page. A person who has been to Williams Sonoma and Crate and Barrel websites is likely to be in the market for house wares, and thus the Pottery Barn might choose to advertise to these consumers when they land on Google search.

Insight about consumers' goals is not only informed by an assessment of their life goals, but also by an evaluation of their momentary psychological states. Consumers might be feeling powerful or powerless, or they may be energized or fatigued. Such momentary psychological states can affect consumers' responses to advertising as well as their brand preferences. Those who experience a feeling of being powerless have a greater desire to acquire status-related items such as Starbucks coffee, or an Armani suit as a means of compensating for their lack of power (see Rucker and Galinsky 2008), and those who are fatigued are likely to spend more when shopping than those who are not depleted (Vohs and Farber 2007).

Although it might seem difficult to identify when these momentary psychological states would occur and thus when a strategy that corresponds to the psychological state is appropriate, there are correlates of these states that enhance prediction. For example, a recession or negative economic news might serve as a predictor of powerlessness, and days of the week (Monday), or time of day (morning for teens, late afternoon for elderly adults) might be a predictor of consumer fatigue and in this way influence their consumption behavior. Furthermore, brands can place their advertisements strategically. Brands wanting to target consumers who are feeling happy might choose to advertise in a comedy rather than a drama. Online, brands with the goal to communicate with consumers when they feel powerless might choose to run their executions alongside news stories that are likely to trigger feelings of powerlessness among consumers. Indeed, DeBeers advertises its diamonds during a recession even though consumers might be conserving resources because this is a time when affluent consumers might feel a need to be empowered.

When the recession hit, Hyundai promised to take back the new car brand purchases, if their financial circumstances did not allow them to make the payments. This strategy is in keeping with the brand's position, which is to minimize consumer risk by devices such as extended warranties. And retailers might hold sales on Mondays when people are feeling a need for a boost in self-esteem after trudging back into the work week.

Stage in the Life Cycle

Individuals' stage in the life cycle affects their goals and thus their beliefs about categories and brands. The goal in conducting life-cycle analysis is to determine whether there is a match between consumers' goals in a particular stage of the life cycle and the benefits delivered by a brand. Consider, for example, how people at different points in their life cycle evaluate automobile choices. Young people and empty nesters (those whose kids have left home) tend to value speed and sportiness highly, whereas those with young children find comfort and safety to be more important in choosing a car. Along these lines, Chrysler found that the PT Cruiser's sportiness was attractive to empty nesters, whereas the Jeep's perceived safety benefits appealed to those with families. Advertising for these brands highlighted these target-relevant features.

The generation in which people grew up also affects their beliefs and motivations that are reflected in their consumption behavior. People who grew up during the depression have different beliefs about products and services than do those who grew up during the Vietnam conflict. Here, we highlight some of the more important generational influences on consumers' beliefs and consumption.

Generation X. Generation X is composed of those in the US born between 1965 and 1978. It includes 45 million people, which is a small cohort when compared to the approximately 78 million baby boomers (born between 1944 and 1964). This was the first generation of latch key children who grew up in dual career households, half of which were single parent homes. Many Gen Xers entered the workforce at a time of downsizing and unemployment. They often feel alienated from the culture and are discouraged about their career path, which is crowded by boomers. Generation Xers tend to spend more on movies, clothing, alcohol, restaurant meals and electronic equipment than do boomers. They aspire to making a lot of money owning a swimming pool and having second homes, but without the expectation of being able to achieve the materialism to which they aspire. Advertising to Generation X should thus situate the brand within this life space.

Generation X reacts poorly to marketing efforts that involve traditional media. Advertising that attracts their attention typically does not appear to be promoting the brand. Nike's "Just Do It" advertising was popular with Generation X because it focused on the activity rather than on enumerating the unique benefits of the brand. Additionally, given Generation Xers' technological savvy, advertising over the internet is an especially effective medium.

Generation Y. Generation Y or echo boomers are the 71 million Americans born between 1979 and 1994, who are the children of baby boomers. They are a racially diverse group in which one out of three individuals is not Caucasian. Seventy-five percent of Gen Yers were raised by a working mother and 25% by a single parent. Gen Yers are characterized by their pragmatism and long-term planning. More than 25% live at home after graduation, in part as a means of saving money and in part to be close to family. Unlike the parents of Generation X kids, who viewed living at home after college graduation as an indication of failure, boomers' parents are often willing to support their kids in an effort to help them achieve their passion. Gen Y views the near term as uncertain and without a necessarily right or wrong path. First jobs are viewed as temporary; they are intended to last less than 3 years. At the same time, from an early age they begin to invest for the long term.

Gen Yers are cynical about traditional mass media. It is not that they do not watch TV, but that they are quite selective in their viewing. Their favorite networks are FOX, NBC, and the Discovery Channel. Gen Yers represent a substantial audience for reality TV. They are attracted to edgier ads that focus on how a brand fits into their life rather than on its attributes. Sprite ads that presented a parody of brand endorsers and carried the tagline "Image is nothing. Obey your thirst" were highly effective in attracting Gen Y consumption.

Similarly, an ad for Arizona jeans that shows teens mocking an ad that attempts to speak their language with the slogan "Just show me the jeans" has helped grow the popularity of this brand among teens.

Bobos. In the past several years, there has been a rapidly growing trend for people to purchase high priced items. For example, $400 Dualit toasters, an industrial strength product that browns toast evenly, have become very popular, as have $20,000 oversized slate shower stalls, road bikes priced at $4000 dollars and top-of-line $300 hiking boots. What is common among these products is that they are functional rather than cosmetic. The notion is that it is virtuous to spend lavishly if the purchases are for functional items. This virtue extends to purchases in categories where people do not make substantial use of the products purchased. Viking ovens and granite countertops are common purchases among those who do little or no cooking. And the products purchased are ones that at one time were quite inexpensive. A $4 cup of coffee or bottle of water, a $5 toothbrush, and $50 T-shirts have attracted substantial demand.

David Brooks has labeled the individuals who engage in the purchase of expensive functional items as Bobos (*Bobos in Paradise*). Bobos are people who have integrated both bourgeois and bohemian values. They value products and brands that allow them to express their individuality. In this way, consumption conforms to bourgeois values. At the same time, these products are utilitarian or functional and thus conform to the anti-materialistic bohemian values. Brooks describes how Bobos reconcile disparate values: "They are prosperous without seeming greedy; they have pleased their elders without seeming conformist; they have risen toward the top without too obviously looking down on those below; they have achieved success without committing certain socially sanctioned affronts to the ideal of social equality; they have constructed a prosperous lifestyle while avoiding the old clichés of conspicuous consumption..." Thus, when advertising to Bobos, two guidelines should be followed: make the brand unique in its category, and represent the category as functional.

Individual Differences

Individuals' age, social class and gender influence their goals, the product benefits they value, and how they process advertising information. Consumer insights provided by each of these individual differences is examined.

Age and Cognitive Development. Age is perhaps the most frequently used variable in segmentation for advertising. Targets are usually described in terms of age categories that are used in the census survey. These include 20-24, 25-29, 30-34 etc... Age is used as an indicator of product and brand usage. In addition, current knowledge about how individuals of particular ages respond to advertising is of value in deciding whether or not segmentation is warranted.

As kids' cognitive development progresses their response to advertising changes. Children under the age of 6 have limited processing abilities. The absence of prior knowledge makes it difficult for these children to elaborate on incoming information or to retrieve the information that they have previously processed. At the same time, the absence of existing knowledge makes memory fertile ground for rote learning and verbatim recall. Young children show an uncanny ability to play back advertising word for word. This is especially the case when information has a problem-episode-outcome structure. Thus, kids under the age of 6 have the ability to learn ad messages verbatim as well as the ability to learn the content of ads that have a story structure. Therefore, advertising to this segment typically involves a problem solution or other story format as it aids in their learning.

Between the ages of six and 10, kids develop the ability to rehearse information so that it is represented in memory, and they have the ability to organize the information they store so that related information is represented at the same location in memory. In addition, this age group exhibits the skill to retrieve related information before accessing information about some disparate topic. However, kids under 10 do not reliably use these skills because they do not activate information storage and retrieval strategies spontaneously. When they are prompted to rehearse incoming information or to retrieve everything they know about one topic before moving to the next, they exhibit adult-like processing and retrieval capabilities, though their capacity is more limited than is that of older people. Children under the age of six are much less affected by such prompts. The implication is that for those aged six to 10, reminding them of the rules for effective processing and retrieval of message information as part of the persuasive appeal is likely to facilitate their later use of message information.

The above analysis suggests ways to enhance the effectiveness of the $900 million spent annually against advertising to kids under 12 in the US. However, more effective kid advertising is not the issue of greatest priority in advertising to kids. It is the threat of government regulation. In the past several years, there has been growing concern that advertising to kids promotes poor nutritional habits. In response, large food producers such as McDonalds, Campbell Soup and PepsiCo have voluntarily stopped advertising on programming viewed predominantly by kids under 12 when the product does not meet certain nutritional specifications. And major advertisers to kids including Kraft, Cadbury, Mars and Kellogg's have opened their marketing plans to the scrutiny of the Better Business Bureau. Whether these initiatives to limit government regulation of kids' advertising will be effective is yet to be determined.

Those 65 and older are often viewed as representing another age segment. Older adults comprise over 12% of the American population. They include the most affluent people in the country. And, they are easily reached via mass media. With the attrition in their life space because of retirement, death of their spouse and cohort members, older adults rely on mass media for information to a greater extent than do their younger counterparts. Yet, with the exception of products that are specifically targeted at the elderly, little marketing attention is devoted to attracting them. Indeed, most marketing plans include people who are 49 years of age or younger. Even when advertising features older people, the appeal often does not reflect an understanding of the elderly consumer. They are treated as if there is one elderly segment. This practice is not consistent with the data suggesting that the knowledge and lifestyles of those under 75 are quite different than their older counterparts.

Elderly, and particularly those under 75, typically view themselves as being healthier and younger than do younger adults. Indeed, the elderly's self-perception is that they are 10-15 years younger than their chronological age. Thus, when advertising is targeted to say a 70-year old, it is appropriate to show a 55-year-old rather than a person who is the same age as the target member.

The conventional wisdom that elderly people's ability to recall information is diminished with age is not supported by evidence. The findings are that older people retain proficiency in previously learned tasks and suffer deficits primarily when the tasks are ones that require skills that have not been learned earlier in life. For example, today's elderly are likely to have a difficult time when television advertising employs quick cuts -- rapid movement from one scene to another. In addition, limitations in learning that do occur generally do not start at age 65, but rather there is a diminution in learning ability that becomes somewhat more pronounced after 45.

Advertising to older adults appears to be most effective when presented through print media because it allows older individuals to process message information at their own pace. Thus, newspapers and magazines are good choices for elderly targets. When older consumers are familiar with a product category, broadcast media are also effective. In addition, about one-third of those 65 and older are currently on the internet and this age cohort represents the fastest growing users. Given the ability to present self-paced information on the internet, this medium is an attractive choice when targeting older consumers.

Social Class. The availability of demographic information, and particularly the educational attainment of the target, can be used to infer social class. This factor might be important to consider as a segmentation variable because there is evidence that social classes differ in the types of offerings and persuasive messages they are likely to find appealing. Upscale people value uniqueness and individuality. Information that emphasizes how a brand may reinforce one's feeling of individuality is particularly appealing to upscale people. Thus, they are more willing than other social class groups to try unknown brands. Middle-class people value neatness and organization. Information that shows convincingly that a product can help achieve these goals is typically well received. In contrast, downscale people value functionality and believe that luck is critical to success. They exhibit greater reliance on major brands than do other social classes, perhaps because they lack confidence in their ability to evaluate alternative offerings and make appropriate brand choices.

It should be noted that upscale people often engage in downscale consumption. They shop at Saks and Dollar stores. By contrast, downscale people typically confine their consumption to downscale products and services. This asymmetry in social class behavior might explain why there is so little advertising targeted to downscale consumers: There is also a market for these products among more upscale individuals and so mass advertising is used for these products.

These observations do not imply that downscale people refrain from buying expensive products. Some downscale people have greater disposable income than do more upscale consumers. This privilege within a class occurs because downscale people tend to underspend for housing and lifestyle activities in relation to their more upscale counterparts. As a result, downscale consumers have the income to purchase high-ticket items. They often do so in categories that represent their aspirations. For example, they were among the first to purchase TVs and color TVs and among the first to buy flat panel TVs.

Social class can be applied not only to consumers, but also to products. Products that are plentiful or used in large quantities and lack potency are considered more downscale than ones that are consumed in small quantities and are potent. For example, in the context of beverages, liqueurs and champagne are perceived to be upscale, whereas beer is perceived to be downscale. Advertising needs to consider the social class of the user as well as the social class of the product category in developing persuasive messages.

Finally, some brands have social class associations. Cartier watches have an upscale association, whereas Timex is more downscale. Science Diet dog food is upscale, whereas Alpo is more downscale. Brands design their marketing strategies to reflect these associations. Along these lines, Levi's dropped its line of coveralls in an effort to elevate the social class of its brand. At the same time, there are brands that are not specifically associated with a particular social class. McDonald's for example is perceived to be relevant to a wide spectrum of social classes.

Gender. There is substantial evidence that, at least under certain circumstances, men and women differ in how they respond to persuasive messages. Women tend to be slower to make decisions, they exhibit greater uncertainty about their decisions, and they are more persuadable. These differences are fostered by how each gender is socialized. Women are encouraged to be communal, which involves a consideration of self and others in decision making. By contrast, men tend to be agentic, which entails a self-expressiveness and goal-directedness.

Support for these characterizations comes from a wide variety of studies. Investigations of children's activities report that boys are frequently asked to go to the store or to achieve some other goal on their own that requires goal-directedness. Girls are often given tasks that require them to coordinate with or navigate among the other members of the household, which enhances the development of their communal skills. Similarly in studies of parent-kid play, such as those involving the solution of puzzles, boys are sent off to complete a part of the puzzle by themselves, which enhances the development of their agency, whereas girls and parents solve the puzzle together, which enhances girls' communal skills. Instructions given to girls are often particular to the task (put the dogs with the dogs and the cats with the cats). In contrast, boys are given more general rules (put things together that share common features). General instructions are likely to be more useful than particular ones when attempting to achieve goals beyond the immediate context and thus promote agency.

It appears that a communal focus enhances women's proclivity to consider two disparate factors, self and others, in making a decision. Thus, women are likely to exhibit community in social interactions by expressing a concern for others as well as self ("isn't it warm in here?"), whereas males' responses tend to be more directed toward achieving their own goals ("turn on the air conditioning"). Applied to message processing tasks, community is manifested by females' tendency to be more detailed processors of disparate bits of information than are men. This difference is manifested in females' greater likelihood of processing message information that includes different types of product benefits than do men. Males' agency often prompts them to focus on the information that they feel is critical to decision making. This may be manifested by their greater reliance on prior knowledge and other heuristics (cognitive shortcuts) as a basis for judgment.

The observation of gender differences in information processing implies that different types of advertising appeals might be more persuasive for men and women. For males, messages that focus on a single benefit are generally more effective. If multiple benefits are to be communicated, a pool of ads is recommended, each featuring a single benefit. For women, the presentation of disparate types of benefits is more appropriate. Advertising directed at making distinctions among the different flankers of a brand available to the consumer is generally welcomed by women, but not by men.

It is important to note that these gender differences emerge in a limited set of circumstances. In many situations, these differences are swamped by contextual factors. Under time pressure, women are likely to invoke the same heuristics as those used by men, and when a decision is important men typically exhibit the same use of disparate types of information as those used by women.

Women's social circumstances also have stimulated change in what motivates their purchases. Seventy-five percent of women are in the workforce, 58% of college graduates are women (vs. 35% in 1960), 33% of women make more than their spouse (vs. 24% in 1987), 40% of business travelers are women (vs. 1% in 1970), and 62% of women under 30 have not been married (vs. 53% in 2000). These changes imply that women today place a high premium on convenience, are likely to exhibit more agency attendant to their empowerment and time famine, are likely to purchase different brands of car and take different vacations than in the past, and look for different qualities in a partner than they did a decade ago.

As is the case for social class, brands often are perceived as either masculine or feminine (Aaker provides a detailed analysis of brand personality). For example, Burger King is perceived to be more masculine than McDonald's, and Nike is seen as more masculine than Reebok. These perceptions reflect the heritage of these brands. Burger King was initially positioned to appeal to the big appetites of men, whereas McDonald's was positioned as the all-family restaurant. Reebok was introduced as a woman's fitness shoe, whereas Nike was marketed as a man's running shoe. When a brand is perceived to be associated with a gender, the impact of advertising can often be enhanced by elaborating on this facet of a brand's imagery. Indeed, Burger King's current campaign has largely focused on reinforcing the masculine equity of the brand with the introduction of their creepy King icon.

Developing a Consumer Insight Statement: Harley-Davidson

We have examined consumer insights about the category and brands and how these insights are influenced by a variety of factors. The product of this analysis is a consumer insight statement, which typically involves the description of the category segments, an assessment of their behaviors and motivations for using the category and an analysis of their attraction to a specific brand. A consumer insight statement is illustrated using the motorcycle category and the Harley-Davidson brand. It is developed on the basis of an ethnography; that is, by researchers who travelled with bikers as a means of observing their behaviors and listening to their views as a basis for inferring their motivations (Schouten and McAlexander 1995). The representation of a consumer insight statement in marketing strategy is illustrated.

The motorcycle category is associated with outlaws. Riders are typically perceived to be individuals attired in black leathers and black boots, sporting long hair, beards, and tattoos, who are known for their machismo. And, while some bike riders conform to this stereotype, as is evident at motorcycle rallies such as those in Sturgis South Dakota, most do not. In fact, riders represent a variety of different segments. Bikers are affluent urban dwellers, suburban weekend riders who are lawyers, accountants, and teachers, retired individuals who tour on bikes, and religious individuals. The core value shared by these groups is a desire for freedom, which takes two forms. One is liberation. This is the freedom from the demands of jobs, family and routines. They contrast the freedom of their bikes to the confinement of a car, which they refer to as a coffin or cage. The other freedom involves license to engage in behaviors that are not sanctioned in their everyday lives. They rankle at the requirement to wear a helmet and restrictions on the noise emitted by their mufflers. Biking offers its users a community that shares these self-transforming values without compromising their conformity to societal values that they live by every day.

Harley-Davidson is the only American producer of motorcycles. Its products are typically larger and less nimble than those of their Japanese competitors (Honda, Suzuki, Yamaha, and Kawasaki). Harley prides itself in being authentic and not changing the basic elements of its bikes. The Harley brand also taps into people's desire for freedom by using a variety of symbols. The fact that the brand features large powerful bikes engenders a masculine image. Because masculinity is associated with agency, that is, self-expression and goal pursuit (vs. association of femininity with community), it is a symbol of freedom. The fact that the brand is American and features an eagle on its products presents additional symbols of freedom. And freedom is also conveyed by associating Harley with a distinctive loud rumbling engine. At the same time, Harley makes an effort to ensure that its riders do not feel like outcasts, by the establishment of a Harley Owners Group (HOG). Within the HOG there is the freedom to associate with those who share the particular form of freedom that is important to the individual, whether it pertains to the demographics, sexual or religious preference, or some other factor.

Advertising for Harley makes use of this insight. Black sheep are shown escaping their pens, leaving the white sheep behind, and going to a city (presumably Sturgis) where the sign welcomes Harley riders. These visuals are accompanied by the Guns N' Roses (GNR) song "Paradise City." GNR and its lead singer, Axl Rose, were known for their rebellious nature, which fits with the goals of the Harley target. And the retro nature of the product is matched by the fact that GNR was popular in the 1980s and Paradise City was released in 1987. The spot was shot in black and white also gives it a retro feel. It can be viewed at:
www.youtube.com/watch?v=sSY0nCuRhHA

Thus, insight about the category and brand are used in the presentation of the product and product-related services. It also guides the development of the brand's position and the creative executions used to convey that position.

Summary of Consumer Insight: What Consumers Think

Consumer insight is based on an analysis of consumers' beliefs about the brand and category. In turn, these beliefs are influenced by lifestyle and momentary goals, consumers stage in the life cycle, the generation into which they were born, and individual difference factors including age, social class and gender. An understanding of consumer beliefs and their origins provides a basis for developing persuasive messages that highlight the link between their goals and the benefits derived by brand purchase and use.

Chapter Exercises

- Consider a brand that you use or that you find interesting that others use the brand and the category in which the brand has membership. What do you think the particular goals are that are served by the category in which the brand holds membership and the brand? That is, what is the psychographic profile of the target? Develop a consumer insight for this category and brand and suggest how the insight might be represented in brand advertising.

- Consider different potential targets for these brands and how you might gear your advertising to them. First, take the role of the brand manager for Lexus automobiles. Can the advertising be specialized to speak to unique insights for men and women? How might this be accomplished strategically and executionally? Now, consider advertising for Walmart versus Target. Historically, Wal-mart has been downscale and Target upscale. How might the advertising for each store best take advantage of insights about social class?

Recommended Readings

Aaker, Jennifer (1997), "Dimensions of Brand Personality," *Journal of Marketing Research*, 34, 347-357.

Brooks, David (2000), *Bobos in Paradise: The New Upper Class and How They Got There*, New York; London: Simon & Schuster

John Schouten and James McAlexander (1995), "Subcultures of Consumption: An Ethnography of the New Bikers," *Journal of Consumer Research, 22,* 43-61.

Rucker, Derek D., and Adam D. Galinsky (2008), "Desire to Acquire: Powerlessness and Compensatory Consumption," *Journal of Consumer Research, 35,* 257-267.

Vohs, Kathleen D., and Ronald J. Faber (2007), "Spent Resources: Self-regulatory Resource Availability Affects Impulse Buying," *Journal of Consumer Research, 33,* 537–547.

Consumer Insight

Processing of Ads

Chapter 4

Chapter 4 Objectives

- Memory and judgment: Cognitive path
  - o Memory organization and positioning
  - o Information retrieval and judgment
  - o Primacy of acceptance
- Metacognitive path
  - o Feelings of ease
  - o Feelings of fit
- Perceptual path

How does advertising work? Consider two consumers, Phil and Beth, at a bar deciding what beer to order. Phil has seen an ad that shows several Corona beers on a dock in the foreground with a tranquil sea as the vista. You can hear people enjoying themselves, but they are not shown. Phil thinks of Mexico because Corona is produced in Mexico and because the water evokes thoughts of an Acapulco beach where he vacationed last winter. The ad reminds Phil of his good friend Derek, who always orders Corona with a lime when they go to a bar. Phil also remembers the refreshing taste of the Corona beer he drank while at the beach in Acapulco. When Phil orders beer, these thoughts about Corona prompt him to request the brand. In contrast, Beth does not rely upon these associations when ordering a beer. Instead, what pops into Beth's head is the image of Corona's long-necked clear bottle that lets her see the golden yellow beer through the bottle. This cue suggests to Beth that the beer is purer than other beers and prompts her to choose Corona.

Although both consumers choose the same beer in this scenario, the paths to persuasion are strikingly different and involve different types of information processing (figure 4.1). Phil's path to persuasion is cognitive. It relies on Phil's associations to Corona beer that are stored in his memory. It is also metacognitive, which refers to the fact that it involves thoughts about thoughts. When Phil reflects on his decision to choose Corona, it feels easy and it feels right; and these positive (metacognitive) feelings about the decision process become associated with Corona. In contrast, Beth's selection of beer is perceptual and thus based on the physical cues of the beer presented at the time of purchase or consumption such as the features of the bottle and color of the beer.

In this chapter, we describe how consumers use advertising information to make decisions and we suggest how this knowledge might be used to influence their judgments. We begin with a discussion of how to affect consumers' judgments based on associations to a brand that are in memory as well as those presented in advertising (cognitive path). This discussion focuses on how advertising messages can influence the associations consumers have to a brand and thereby impact their behavior. We also examine how the manner in which the message is framed influences feelings about the decision process and thus judgments of the brand message (metacognitive path). Finally, we assess how advertising might affect persuasion through the perceptual path.

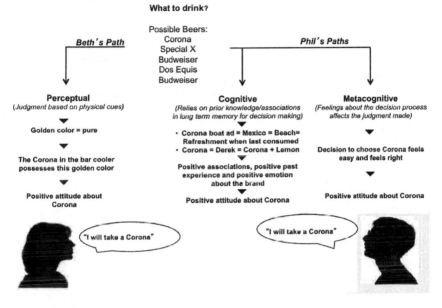

Figure 4.1: Three Paths to Decision Making

Memory and the Judgment Process:
The Cognitive Path to Persuasion

As a starting point in developing advertising strategies to influence consumers' behavior, we review the two-stage memory model of information processing developed in **Chapter 2**. This model is depicted in figure 4.2. When a consumer is exposed to an ad, the information received is represented in short-term memory, which is what a person is thinking about at the moment (labeled **#1** in figure 4.2). This information might consist of new information learned about Corona from the advertisement as well as associations to Corona retrieved from long-term memory. From these sources, the information in short-term memory might be related to brand attributes (e.g., Corona is thirst quenching), information about the occasion of use (e.g., Corona is perfect for a hot day), or some emotion (e.g., drinking a Corona is relaxing; **#2**, figure 4.2).

Because short-term memory is limited in capacity this store can only accommodate a small amount of information for a brief period of time. For new information to be stored for later use in long term memory or to reinforce prior information by creating stronger associations, individuals must engage in amplification. Amplification occurs when we process information on a deeper level. More enduring memories are created when we try to relate information to past knowledge or experiences in long-term memory (**#3**, figure 4.2). The extent of amplification (the deeper we think about something and number of connections that we can make) influences the number and strength of associations that people have to a brand. When consumers evaluate a brand, they rely on relevant information that is accessible in memory. The extent to which information has been amplified and was recently processed enhances its accessibility, retrieval, and representation in short-term memory and its use in making a decision (**#4**, figure 4.2).

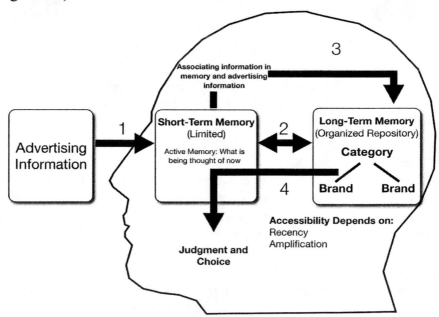

Figure 4.2: The Cognitive Path to Persuasion

In the Corona example described earlier, the ad, which conveyed the idea that Corona was refreshing, prompted Phil to think about Corona, which made him think of Mexico and the Acapulco beach where the Corona he drank was refreshing (figure 4.3). Thus, the Corona ad claim that Corona was refreshing was amplified by its association to prior knowledge that Phil had in long-term memory. This amplification made the belief that Corona was refreshing accessible when Phil was ordering a beer.

An important implication of the information processing and judgment model is that consumers store not only message information, but also *their own* idiosyncratic responses to an advertisement and activate *their own* repertoire of message-relevant information during the retrieval stage. While advertising might help inform the consumer about a brand, it is consumers' own response to, and interpretation of an advertisement that affects their behavior. Thus, a cell phone carrier might promote its great coverage by stating that it operates in six of the seven continents. However, rather than encoding that the service has great coverage message, consumers might infer and remember that the service was incomplete.

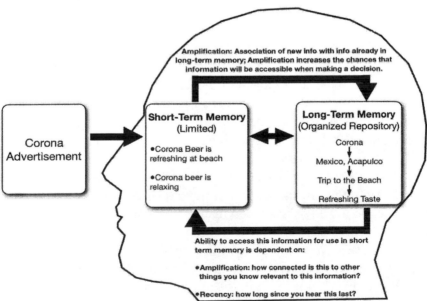

Figure 4.3: The Cognitive Path to Persuasion Applied to Corona

The observation that advertising ultimately relies on self-persuasion has several implications for advertisers. First, as we noted in **Chapter 2**, it suggests that initial consideration should be given to targeting advertising at current users of the category and brand. Users are likely to have favorable dispositions toward the category and brand they use, and thus are likely to be more easily convinced by advertising for it than nonusers because they have more positive associations already formed. Second, the view that much of persuasion is self-persuasion implies that advertising has little hope of saving a poor product. Even if the advertising leads consumers to form an initially positive impression of a brand, disconfirmation during product use will likely undermine future usage. Third, when a brand offers important benefits to the consumer, the extent to which consumers' judgments are influenced by this information depends on its amplification, that is, the number and strength of the associations to the brand. This observation underscores the importance of introducing and utilizing creative strategies that facilitate amplification of message information.

The Effect of Different Levels of Amplification

Consumers engage in different levels of amplification (see Petty and Cacioppo, 1986). Imagine a billboard for a furniture store that presents a picture of an attractive spokesperson as well as a list of several relevant brand attributes (e.g., fine craftsmanship, exotic woods, etc...). In one instance, a consumer might drive past the billboard and give it only a quick glance. She does not have time to amplify the message to any great extent. What the consumer did notice was the celebrity spokesperson and the list of features on the billboard. Even though she might not have read any of features listed or thought about the spokesperson featured, the mere endorsement of the spokesperson and the fact that there are numerous reasons to shop at the furniture store might affect store evaluation. We refer to the use of shortcuts that involve the reliance of peripheral cues such as the number of arguments made or the attractiveness of the source as *heuristics*. Examples of heuristics in this case might be "if a celebrity is endorsing the store, the store must sell high quality items," or "there are ten reasons to shop at this store, so it must be a worthwhile to stop in." Heuristics involve little amplification, and thus require limited effort. Often times the information relied upon for heuristic thinking (such as source attractiveness) would be considered irrelevant if given more thought.

In contrast, another consumer stopping at the same light might take more time to look at the billboard. As this person reads through the list of features, she evaluates each of them with respect to their relevance. Because the features are relevant to her, a favorable impression of the furniture store is formed. Similar to the earlier Corona example, both consumers arrive at a similar conclusion (positive attitude) despite using different bits of information and amplifying this information to different degrees.

Of course, consumers are not forced to rely solely on either message arguments or heuristic cues; they can utilize both. However, the relative importance of each in influencing consumers' evaluations varies with the amount of amplification done; the greater the amplification, the less the reliance on heuristics. Furthermore, it is not necessarily the case that amplification leads to more favorable brand evaluations than heuristic processing, but it is the case the more amplification leads to more lasting impressions. If the billboard featured a celebrity spokesperson accompanied by a long list of irrelevant features, those relying on heuristics might be more favorable towards the advertised brand than those who amplified by scrutinizing the arguments. This outcome is anticipated because the celebrity spokesperson and the fact that there were many brand features listed would be highly persuasive to the heuristic processor (celebrity=quality; numerous attributes=good place to shop), whereas those who amplified the feature information might have been unfavorable because the arguments for brand purchase were not perceived to be compelling (perhaps the billboard mentioned attributes such as a newly painted store or ample motorcycle parking). These observations suggest that brands offering strong arguments to support their use will benefit from increasing the amount of message amplification, whereas amplification of irrelevant reasons will unfavorably affect the consumer's opinion ("this store has nothing that appeals to me"). However, if consumers are not expected to pay significant attention to an ad, perhaps because of the context in which it is presented as described in the billboard example, an effort should be made to enhance the impact of heuristic cues that will serve as the basis for judgments, such as number of reasons, celebrity endorsements or expert opinions.

The Use of Cognitive Resources in Amplification

As noted earlier, in situations where thoughtful attention is expected to enhance brand evaluation, efforts should be made to prompt amplification. For this to occur, it is important that the message information be relevant to consumers' goals. Amplification also requires that substantial resources (such as interest and time) are available to process message information; otherwise heuristic processing will occur. Assuming that these resources are available, consumers evaluate whether a message warrants the allocation of the resources. Certain variables affect this decision. Factors such as message repetition **(Chapter 8)** and the use of humor and threat in an appeal **(Chapter 9)** might be used to stimulate the allocation of resources that are required for message amplification. A detailed discussion of the role of resources in amplification of message information is presented by Petty and Cacioppo (1986).

Resources and acceptance. Intuitively, it would seem that as the resources necessary to process a message become available, consumers first must pay attention to advertising and understand it. Once they understand it, they either accept the view advocated in the message if the information is viewed as compelling, or reject the appeal if it judged to be unbelievable. Acceptance results in a favorable attitude toward the brand, intention to purchase, and ultimately purchase and consumption when consumers are motivated and have the ability to act on their disposition. This is referred to as the Cartesian view because it has its origins in the work of René Descartes.

As reasonable as this conceptualization appears to be, the emerging evidence favors the Spinozan view, which suggests that affirmation is primary. When information is relevant, people accept the message advocacy as believable as a means of understanding the information presented and only reject after acceptance if the message is found to not be believable upon further consideration. Thus in contrast to the Cartesian view, acceptance is an inherent aspect of comprehension. People might act upon this information or they might scrutinize it further in relation to other information they have stored in memory (i.e., amplification) to determine whether to reject a message advocacy. However, in situations of limited resources, where consumers lack the cognitive resources and/or time to further evaluate the information after acceptance, the message is judged to be true. A detailed discussion of the primacy of affirmation is developed by Gilbert (1991) and further discussed by Grant and Colleagues (2004).

The Spinozan view has important implications when messages include negations such as "It's not your father's Oldsmobile," "It's not delivery, its DiGiorno," and "no added sugar." It suggests that people process information in two parts. They first process the affirmation as a means of acceptance and if enough resources are available, they then process the negator "not." Thus, message recipients who are told there is "no added sugar" might initially process "added sugar" rather than "no added sugar" if they have enough resources to amplify the affirmation but not the negator. This inference of "added sugar" is the opposite of the one intended. And this outcome can occur even if people have the correct negator stored in memory, but it is not sufficiently amplified to be accessible when thinking about a claim that includes a negation. When additional resources are allocated to processing the message, the negator will also be accessed and recall of the claim will be accurate.

The case of too many resources. It might appear that to ensure that message recipients process a message accurately, the more resources available the better. However, this is not the case. The availability of more resources than are needed for message processing can prompt a level of amplification that undermines the persuasive impact of a message. When the information is new, thought is focused on learning the message content; however, after consumers have encountered the message numerous times, there is no longer anything to learn from the message per se. Thoughts thus might focus on other information that would help in making a judicious decision, such as past experiences with the product. These thoughts are typically not as positive as those generated directly from the message, which is de-

signed to be persuasive. The result is that after a point, repeated exposure to an ad might result in the activation of consumers' own idiosyncratic thoughts, reducing the persuasive impact of the appeal. For
example, in one experiment those who had seen the same McDonald's ad many times no longer thought about the features described
in the message, as people who had seen only a few exposures had reported. Instead, these individuals activated idiosyncratic thoughts. For
example, one individual reported thinking about a fly he found in a
burger when he had worked at McDonald's. In other instances, the
idiosyncratic thoughts might take the form of "I already know what
they are saying." Both of these thoughts are less favorable toward a
brand and thus undermine persuasion compared to arguments expressed in a brand message, which is designed specifically with the
intent to persuade. Of course, not all idiosyncratic thoughts are negative. For example, for a favorite brand these thoughts might be no less
favorable than the information presented in the message, in which
case repeated exposure would not undermine persuasion.

This discussion raises the issue of what strategies are appropriate when the target is composed of people who are familiar with
the product compared versus unfamiliar with the product. One approach to responding to this dilemma is to present the functional benefit and at the same time include news for those who are familiar with
the brand. Along these lines, BMW might discuss safety in terms of
anti-lock brakes in one advertisement, crash test results in another,
and traction control in yet another advertisement.

The persuasive effect of amplification can thus be somewhat
uncertain. It depends on what is amplified. However, there are reliable outcomes that occur when consumers amplify message information based on strong arguments and points of differences.
Amplification solidifies people's thoughts about a brand. Their judgments tend to be more accessible and held with greater confidence as
amplification increases. As a result, attitudes formed through amplification tend to be more likely to persist over time, resist change, and
influence behavior. When strong arguments exist, it is of value to motivate people to recruit the resources needed for message amplification. A detailed discussion of how amplification affects confidence is
presented by Rucker and Petty (2006).

Judgments Based on the Metacognitive Path

The cognitive path to persuasion involves processing message content and relating it to one's own knowledge. Engaging in such processing often produces a subjective experience that also influences brand judgments. This feeling about the process by which a judgment is made is termed metacognitive because it involves thoughts about the process by which a judgment is made rather than thoughts about the message content. Thus, brand evaluations depend not only on what is known about a brand, but also the feelings about how that knowledge was acquired. For example, a consumer who thinks they have processed information in a careful manner (metacognitive path), even if in reality the actual processing is shallow and heuristic (cognitive path), will be more confident in the resulting judgments and thus will behave differently than a consumer who believes they have not carefully processed a message, even if their processing was substantial. We examine several different metacognitions to illustrate how these associations affect judgments.

Feelings of Ease

Consider two executions for BMW. One ad requests that you think of 2 reasons to purchase a BMW, the other requests you think of 10 reasons to purchase a BMW. Which one will result in more favorable evaluations of this brand? If the message recipient takes the cognitive path and focuses on the relevant reasons that they self-generate, she would be more persuaded by coming up with 10 rather than 2 reasons as such successful amplification is likely to make people more favorable. In contrast, if the recipient takes the metacognitive path and focuses on the ease or difficulty of generating these reasons, she will be more favorable when she is asked to think of two reasons. Having to think of 10 reasons will require significant retrieval effort and be perceived as difficult. This feeling will imply that it must be that BMWs are not that good or it would be easy to think of 10 reasons to purchase the car. This process is metacognitive in that brand evaluations depend on the feeling about the judgment process and not on the reasons generated, which is cognitive.

These alternative outcomes raise the question of when people will use a cognitive path and when they will use a metacognitive path. When message recipients believe they know a lot or a little about the advertised brand they adopt the cognitive path. In these cases, feelings about how easy or difficult it is to make a decision are not informative to them and thus they focus on the message content. This is because if much is known about BMW, people already know that generating reasons will be easy and if they know little, they know that generating reasons will be difficult. When message recipients are uncertain about how difficult it is to generate reasons, they focus on this metacognition as a basis for their brand evaluation and perceptions of ease or fluency determine judgments. Tybout and colleagues (2005) discuss the effects of ease in detail. These findings suggest that metacognitions are unlikely to be used by those who have substantial experience with a brand or category or who are at point of entry into a category. Infrequent users of a category are more likely to rely on metacognitions in evaluating a brand.

Feelings of Fit

Brand evaluations are also metacognitive when there is a fit between individuals' goals and the means of goal pursuit represented in the message. By goals we mean self-regulatory goals. Self-regulation refers to internally initiated strategies, such as planning, monitoring against some standard, and evaluating progress, which are implemented in the pursuit of personal goals. People make progress toward their desired outcomes by following a particular strategy. One strategy involves adopting a prevention focus. This focus entails being vigilant and oriented toward safety and security, with an inclination to limit the chances of making mistakes and incurring losses. In contrast, those with a promotion focus adopt an eagerness strategy in their pursuit of accomplishment and growth. Persuading those with each of these goal orientations requires a message that represents goal pursuit in a manner that fits with the goal orientation. When fit occurs, people have an experience of feeling right and engagement that influences their brand judgments.

To illustrate the process, consider a study reported by Angela Lee and Jennifer Aaker (2004). Participants' self-regulatory goal was manipulated by having them read information indicating that grape juice helps prevent disease (prevention-focused), or offers greater energy (promotion-focus). Thus, the category became associated with either promotion or prevention. Subsequently, participants were exposed to a message for the grape juice that included a tagline designed to be associated with either gains or non-losses. The expectation was that those with a prevention focus would find the non-loss message (i.e., "Don't Miss Out on Getting Energized!") to fit better with their safety orientation, whereas those with a promotion focus would experience greater fit when the tagline emphasized information that was consistent with their accomplishment orientation ("Get Energized"). This fit would create a feeling of engagement that resulted in more extreme evaluations of the message. Because the message was an advocacy for the grape juice, this greater extremity would take the form of more positive evaluations. These outcomes were exactly what Lee and Aaker found. Prevention focused individuals were more favorable toward a product when the tagline emphasized not missing out on greater energy, whereas those with a promotion focus were more favorable to the product when the tagline was about getting energized.

Fit has also been found for other means of goal pursuit. For example, those with a prevention focus exhibit more favorable judgments when the message allows for easy comparison, whereas those with a promotion focus are more persuaded when the message presents a sense of locomotion (i.e., a sense of movement towards a goal). This is because comparison is perceived as a way to limit errors of omission, which are important to those with a prevention focus, and locomotion is perceived as an indicator of movement toward accomplishment of a goal. Easy comparison can be achieved by presenting information comparing the target and alternative brands on a series of features all at once, whereas locomotion might be introduced by presenting the same information about the two brands, but presenting a few features at a time to create locomotion. This finding is consistent with the notion that an all at once presentation enhances a feeling of safety by allowing easy comparison, whereas adding features sequentially in a presentation is consistent with the promotion goal of accomplishment by introducing new information.

Along similar lines, prevention-focused individuals are more persuaded by a message when the information presented is concrete (e.g., this car gets 60 miles per gallon) rather than abstract (this car has good gas mileage), because concrete information ensures a knowledge of precisely what was offered, whereas those with a promotion focus are more persuaded by abstract information because it allows them more freedom to imagine the various ways in which the product might lead to goal achievement. These fit findings are developed in greater detail by Malaviya and Sternthal (2009) and Lee and colleagues (2010).

This analysis underscores the importance of identifying situations when a promotion or prevention goal is likely to be activated. Cultural background is one factor that influences goal orientation. Individuals from interdependent cultures (e.g., China) are likely to favor a prevention focus because they place high value on safety and security, whereas those from an independent culture (e.g., America) typically adopt a promotion focus because they put a premium on accomplishment. The consumption context is another factor that might influence the goal orientation adopted. During a recession, people are more likely to adopt a prevention rather than a promotion focus and adopt the opposite orientation when economic conditions are strong.

Momentary psychological needs might also trigger a regulatory orientation. In particular, threats to individuals' identities, sense of power, and self-esteem can activate motives to alleviate such states. As one example, Derek Rucker and Adam Galinsky (2008, 2009) induced people to perceive themselves in either a low or high power state where power is defined as control over one's own or others resources or desired outcomes. These individuals were exposed to a print advertisement for a pen and other products that were associated either with high status or with superior functionality. Low power consumers held more favorable attitudes towards the product framed in terms of status, compared to consumers in a high power or baseline condition. In contrast, when in a state of high power, consumers held more favorable attitudes towards the product framed in terms of functionality compared to both low power and baseline conditions. Moreover, people were willing to pay more when products were advertised as appealing to their needs. Thus, a momentary feeling of low power stimulated people to bolster their sense of power. Because of the need to feel more empowered or to restore their sense of power, individuals were willing to pay more for a product than those who felt powerful. These findings are reviewed in detail in Rucker and Galinsky (2008, 2009).

The Perceptual Path to Persuasion

In some situations, consumers rely on perceptions of thin slices of information as a basis for judgment. For example, they might quickly select the gold and brown package when purchasing chocolate morsels, without knowing the brand name. In these situations, information that is in memory plays a much more limited role than what we have depicted in describing the cognitive path to persuasion.

Perceptual processing also occurs in advertising where just the brand name or a brand icon is shown. This type of information abounds in the form of billboards, signage at sporting events, Internet advertising, product placements and the like. What impact does this information have? Typically, people exhibit poor learning of such advertising when learning is measured by prompts such as "Can you remember seeing an ad for beer?" or "Can you remember seeing an ad for Corona beer?" Yet when consumers who have seen such advertising are asked to indicate their brand choice, they are more likely to select an advertised brand than if they had not been exposed to the advertising. We refer to this memory as perceptual memory. Like memory that is based on the amplification of information, perceptual memory can stimulate persuasion. After perceptual processing of an ad, the brand seems more familiar than it would otherwise. This familiarity is often misattributed to liking, which prompts a greater likelihood of brand purchase than in the absence of the advertising.

If perceptual memory does not involve amplification, how is it enhanced? Research by Angela Lee suggests that one important factor in enhancing perceptual memory is repeated presentation of a brand name. In turn, this sense of familiarity or perceptual fluency increases the likelihood of the brand's selection. For example, suppose that prior to visiting a store you have seen repeatedly the logo for Dr Pepper. This exposure occurred through media advertising, signage at sporting events and product placements in movies. When making a choice at the store, the Dr. Pepper brand appears highly familiar and this familiarity fosters a feeling of liking and helps to reduce feelings of uncertainty. The result is that you are more likely to buy Dr. Pepper than in the absence of these repeated brand name exposures. Of course, this preference might be overcome if consumers amplify on the benefits of a brand other than Dr. Pepper (i.e., the cognitive route); however, the sheer number of decisions to be made in the market place limits the extent to which consumers are willing to engage in such amplification. A detailed discussion of perceptual processing is presented by Lee (2002).

The analysis of the perceptual path to persuasion suggests persuasion via this path is likely to benefit from Internet advertising where consumers might devote little time to attending advertising in the form of banner ads and pop-ups but are exposed to a significant number of ads for a brand. For example, a Maytag ad might appear on a search vehicle such as Google. In addition, advertising for Maytag is presented using a banner ad on Best Buy real estate, an ad on You Tube and a page on a social network such as Facebook. These repeated exposures can enhance familiarity, liking, and certainty, and increase the chances that the brand is considered when making a washer and dryer purchase. And this outcome might occur even if consumers exhibit no awareness of seeing the ad. Of course, the viability of this approach will depend on the extent to which consumers are willing to spend time thinking about competitive advertising that contains strong arguments. In such cases, mere familiarity might be trumped by compelling reasons to purchase a competitor's offering.

Summary of Consumer Insight: Processing of Ads

The current chapter examined the process by which consumers make decisions. An important distinction has been made among three paths to persuasion: Cognitive, metacognitive and perceptual. Each can be a powerful persuasive device. The nature of each path and their triggers are summarized in table 4.1.

Three Paths to Persuasion		
Path to Persuasion	Nature of Processing	Factors Needed to Occur
Cognitive	Association of ad information with consumers' prior knowledge	High Involvement Amplification
	Reliance on heuristics (e.g., number of arguments)	Low involvement Presence of heuristics
Metacognitive	Assessment of the process by which a judgment was made	Ambiguity about brand's value from an assessment of brand knowledge
Perceptual	Quick assessment of perceptual cues including brand name, color, and iconography	Repetition of the icon

Table 4.1: Three Paths to Persuasion

Chapter Exercises

- A restaurant is designing a new direct mail campaign for consumers in their local area. The restaurant features casual dining and affordable prices. The brand has developed two executions. The first execution talks about the restaurant as "not expensive" and "not pretentious." The second execution talks about the restaurant as "affordable" and "casual." Consider the argument that acceptance is primary. Does the proposed tagline make a difference? Building on this, are there any advertising campaigns that might have benefited or been impeded based on this insight about human memory?

- Consider the argument that there is an optimal level of amplification. How might an advertiser assess the optimal level of amplification for an advertisement and/or control the level of amplification? Imagine a company is marketing a high end laptop and has determined that one target group (e.g., college students) will engage in a great deal of message-relevant amplification, whereas another group (e.g., parents) will engage in a relatively cursory processing of the advertisement. How might the company tailor each of their executions to best resonate with the target group based on differences in amplification?

- A vitamin company has two different product lines. The first product line is for a multi-vitamin that has typically been targeted to adults in their early 20's as a means of improving their health. The second product consists of calcium tablets and has been targeted to adults 50+ in order to manage osteoporosis. How would you position each brand based on notions discussed in the meta-cognitive path and fit? Next, imagine each of the following two scenarios. In the first scenario there is a major news story that a steady consumption of vitamins reduces the average number of visits an individual has to take to the doctor. In the second scenario a popular multi-vitamin is recalled due to unattended side effects. What consequences would the scenarios have for the multi-vitamin product?

Recommended Readings

Dubois, David, Derek D. Rucker, Adam D. Galinsky (2010), "The Accentuation Bias: Money Literally Looms Larger (and Sometimes Smaller) to the Powerless," *Social Psychological and Personality Science, 3*, 199-205.

Gilbert, Daniel T. (1991), "How Mental Systems Believe," *American Psychologist, 46,* 107-119.

Grant, Susan Jung, Prashant Malaviya, and Brian Sternthal (2004), "The Influence of Negation on Product Evaluations," *Journal of Consumer Research*, 31, 583-591.

Lee, Angela Y., (2002), "Effects of Implicit Memory on Memory-Based versus Stimulus-Based Brand Choice," *Journal of Marketing Research,* 39(4), 440-454.

Lee, Angela Y. and Jennifer L. Aaker (2004), "Bringing the Frame into Focus: The Influence of Regulatory Fit on Processing Fluency and Persuasion," *Journal of Personality and Social Psychology,* 86(2), 205-218.

Lee, Angela Y (2010), Punam Keller and Brian Sternthal, "Value from Regulatory Construal Fit: The Persuasive Impact of Fit between Consumer Goals and Message Concreteness," *Journal of Consumer Research.*

Malaviya, Prashant and Brian Sternthal (2009), "Parity Product Features can Enhance or Dilute Brand Evaluation: The Influence of Goal Orientation and Presentation Format," *Journal of Consumer Research,* 36, 112-121.

Petty, Richard E., and John T. Cacioppo (1984), "The Effects of Involvement on Responses to Argument Quantity and Quality: Central and Peripheral Routes to Persuasion," *Journal of Personality and Social Psychology, 46,* 69-81.

Petty, Richard E., and John T. Cacioppo (1986), The Elaboration Likelihood Model of persuasion. In L. Berkowitz (Ed.), *Advances in experimental social psychology* (Vol. 19, pp. 123-205). New York: Academic Press.

Rucker, Derek D., and Adam D. Galinsky (2008), "Desire to Acquire: Powerlessness and Compensatory Consumption," *Journal of Consumer Research, 35,* 257-267.

Rucker, Derek D., and Adam D. Galinsky (2009), "Conspicuous Consumption versus Utilitarian Ideals: How Different Levels of Power Shape Consumer Behavior," *Journal of Experimental Social Psychology, 45(3),* 515-523.

Rucker, Derek D., and Richard E. Petty (2006), "Increasing Effectiveness of Communications to Consumers: Recommendations Based on the Elaboration Likelihood and Attitude Certainty Perspectives," *Journal of Public Policy and Marketing,* 25 (1), 39-52.

Tybout, Alice, M., Brian Sternthal, Prashant Malaviya, Yiorgos Bakamitsos, and See-Bum Park (2005), "Information Accessibility as a Moderator of Judgments," *Journal of Consumer Research,* 32, 76-85.

Chapter 5

Brand Positioning

FOR & POD

Chapter 5 Objectives

- Describe the elements of a brand positioning statement
- Discuss various types of frames of reference (FOR) and the rationale for their selection
- Evaluate alternative points of difference (POD) strategies in relation to brand objectives
- Describe tools for evaluating brand value and brand positioning

In 1972, Phil Knight and Bill Bowerman (Knight's former track coach) marketed the first Nike shoe. It had a waffle sole that Bowerman developed using the family waffle iron. This running shoe provided better traction and more cushioning than was available from competitive shoes. To promote Nike shoes, the premier middle and long-distance runner of that time, Steve Prefontaine, was hired as a spokesman. By 1974, the Nike Waffle was the best selling training shoe in the U.S. Several years later, Nike established Athletics West, a facility for the Olympic training of world class athletes. This history is captured in Nike's brand position statement: For those engaging in athletics, Nike provides authentic athletic footwear that enhances athletic performance because it is designed by professionals for professionals. The position has been sustained over time by world class athletes such as John McEnroe, Michael Jordan, and Tiger Woods, and by developing state of the art footwear featuring NIKE-AIR® cushioning. The brand's personality is aggressive and innovative in pursuit of outstanding performance.

The Nike scenario identifies the five key elements of a brand positioning statement:

The target: Those participating in sports
Frame of reference: Athletic footwear
Point(s) of difference: Superior performance
Reason(s) to believe: The professional heritage of Bowerman, Knight, Prefontaine, and current sports stars, as well as the Athletics West facility and the unique shoe construction
Brand personality: Aggressive and innovative

In this chapter, we shall examine how a brand position is developed and articulated through a brand positioning statement and how positioning is made operational in advertising. This entails examining fundamental characteristics of a brand position and then the strategic application of its two key elements—frame of reference and point of difference. We will also discuss brand personality archetypes.

Fundamentals of Brand Positioning

As we noted in describing Nike's position, a brand positioning statement typically involves reporting its five elements: a target, a frame of reference, points of difference, reason to believe, and brand personality. For example, Volvo's positioning statement might read:

> For people with families (*target*), Volvo is the family car (*frame of reference*) that offers the best balance in safety and durability (*points of difference*) because Volvo has a history of intelligent design (*reason to believe*). Volvo is family-oriented, genuine, and old-fashioned (*brand personality*).

The same elements of a positioning statement are employed in a business-to-business context. For example, consider the following positioning statement for Grainger:

> For large corporate customers and individual contractors who purchase industrial maintenance supplies and equipment (*target*), Grainger is the maintenance, repair and operations firm (*frame of reference*) that keeps your business running smoother than other firms (*point of difference*) because it has the largest inventory of industrial supplies (*reason to believe*) that are delivered in a friendly and reliable manner (*brand personality*).

A brand's position can also be depicted schematically, reflecting how information is organized in memory. As we described in our discussion of how people process information **(Chapter 4)**, memory is organized hierarchically; thus a brand and its competitors are thought of as members of a particular category. Using this idea of hierarchical organization, brands positioning can be depicted in terms of a triangle shown in figure 5.1. This representation of how information is organized in memory suggests that the frame of reference is the relationship between a brand and a category. The frame identifies the goal in using the brand. The point of difference reflects how the brands are distinguished from each other. Both the frame of reference and the point of difference can be supported by reasons to believe.

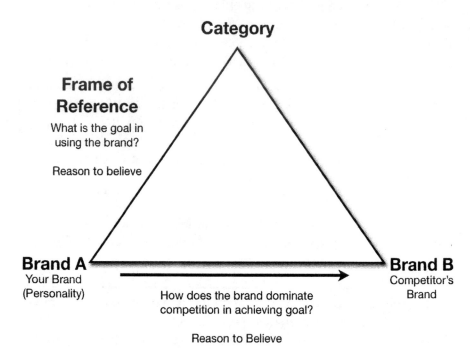

Figure 5.1: The Positioning Triangle

As we noted in the Volvo positioning statement, the frame of reference might be family sedans and the competition might include any number of brands such as Honda, Toyota, Nissan and Buick. The price, size and features of the Volvo might be high-lighted to qualify it as a member of the family sedan category. And features, such as front and side airbags, a crumple zone at the front of the car, uni-construction body, reinforced roof, as well as government crash test results, might be reasons to believe Volvo's superior safety (figure 5.2). Thus, reasons to believe are tangible elements that support the plausibility of a functional or emotional benefit.

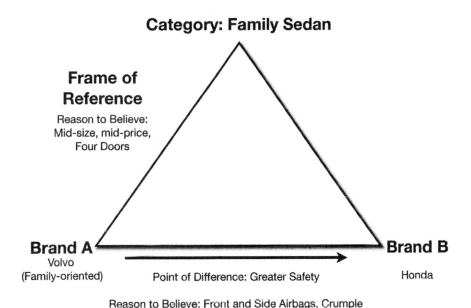

Figure 5.2. The Positioning Triangle for Volvo

Strategic Use of the Frame of Reference

In presenting a brand's position to consumers, the recommended approach is to present the frame of reference first. Consumers need to know what goal can be achieved by using the brand before they can assess how the brand dominates the alternatives against which it competes. Thus, it is important to know that Nike makes athletic shoes if consumers are to appreciate this brand's superior performance. For established brands, the frame of reference and point of difference can be presented together, whereas when a brand is new it is prudent to initially inform consumers about its frame of reference in some detail. Once consumers know what function a brand serves, its point of difference can be described in detail.

The frame of reference is a strategic tool that specifies the goal achieved by a brand and thus suggests the brand's competitive set and the points of difference that might be appropriate. Although the most obvious frame of reference is the category in which the brand holds membership, a brand often competes with members of another category that achieve the same goal. Consider the frames of reference shown in figure 5.3 that Red Bull Cola might select in introducing this product. The brand is a high energy cola. But the frame of reference is not confined to the category in which a brand holds membership (cola). It can be related to other categories (nonalcoholic beverages) or simply to goals (psychological refreshment). And, the potential point of difference or advantage might vary as a function of the frame of reference. This raises the question of when should a specific category be used to communicate the frame of reference and when should a more general goal be used?

Frame of Reference ➡	Potential Competitors ➡	Potential Points of Difference
Cola	Coke, Pepsi, RC Cola	Strong and natural
Natural Refreshment	Snapple, Juice	Energizing
Energy Drink	Monster, Amp	Distinct cola flavor
Non-Alcoholic Beverage	Lemonade, Iced Tea	Great taste
Liquid Refreshment	Water, Gatorade	Maximum revitalization
Psychological Refreshment	Gym, A Walk Outside, Yoga	Convenience

Figure 5.3: Red Bull's Alternative Frames of Reference

Addressing this question requires the consideration of what consumers know about the brand. When a brand is new, consumers generally require highly concrete information about the goal in using a brand. When iPhone was introduced, the frame of reference was a phone and then an iPod. Once consumers apprehended these functions, a list of additional iPod functions were specified, such as downloading information from the internet. In contrast, when developing a frame of reference for an established product, it might be appropriate to consider the goal that the brand achieved in general terms. Encyclopedia Britannica viewed its competition as other encyclopedias. It attempted to find a point of difference that would allow it to dominate Encyclopedia Americana, and the Worldbook Encyclopedia. But consumers viewed encyclopedias as a means of empowering their kids, which meant that computers and the internet were Encyclopedia Britannica's main competition. The failure to use this more abstract frame resulted in Britannica choosing points of difference on which it dominated other encyclopedias (updated more often), but that underscored the brand's deficiencies in relation to the Internet. When planning for an established brand, consideration should be given to the abstract goal that a brand helps consumers accomplish and develop points of difference that allow it to compete with these alternatives.

Representing the Frame of Reference

There are a variety of ways to represent a brand's frame of reference in advertising. The most common approach is to use the category in which the brand holds membership to signify the goal achieved by using the brand. However, the frame of reference can also be communicated using an exemplar or points of parity. We examine the role of each of these approaches.

Category association. When the frame of reference is described in terms of its category membership, several alternatives are typically available. For example, we identified the family car category as Volvo's frame of reference. However, a more inclusive frame such as cars might have been chosen, or a more focused frame such as mid-priced family sedans might have been selected. The preferred category frame is one that provides a substantial target and at the same time enables the brand to be differentiated from competition. Sometimes this means a broader category is more attractive and at other times a narrow frame is more profitable.

To illustrate the virtue of an inclusive frame, consider the strategy developed by Lever 2000. This brand is positioned as a deodorant soap that offers more complete care because its hydrating formula moisturizes the skin. This frame of reference placed Lever 2000 in a category as the only complete bar soap (deodorant *and* moisturizing) and lumped the other deodorant bar soaps into a single function (incomplete care) category. Lever 2000 was thus very successful by adopting a frame that was inclusive of smaller frames of reference. In a category where other brands had covered various niche frames of reference such as moisturizing and deodorizing, it made sense for

Lever to adopt a broad position because this made its point of difference, "does it all," clear to consumers.

Efforts to present a clear and distinct position can also lead to the adoption of a narrow frame of reference. When The Movie Channel (TMC) launched its brand, competitors such as HBO, Cinemax and Showtime were touting the fact that they not only offered movies, but also other programming including concerts and comedy shows. To differentiate itself, TMC used a movie channel frame of reference and conveyed to its audience that its focus on movies made it the one movie channel worth paying for because their focus allowed them to have more of the movies people wanted to see. In this case, the competition had adopted a broad position of entertainment, which provided an opportunity for TMC to compete using a narrow frame. And like TMC, small brands that have a limited business often try to use a limited frame as a basis for their point of differentiation: "We make a better product (e.g., PCV valves) because this is the only thing we make." By using a narrow frame a brand can specialize and compete in a category they have a good chance of owning.

For some brands, several different categories might be plausible as frames of reference at the same point in time. Arm & Hammer baking soda is positioned as a cooking ingredient. But it also is used as a deodorizer that provides a fresh smell when left open in the refrigerator or poured down the drain of sinks or tubs.

Exemplar. Another approach to representing the frame of reference involves the use of an exemplar. An exemplar is a member of the category in which the brand holds membership that consumers associate with a specific benefit. Thus, exemplars provide an efficient means of communicating a specific goal that typically might be more poorly communicated by mere category association. For example, when Subaru promoted the safety of its cars, advertising stated that, "if you liked Volvo consider Subaru." Although these brands are not sold at the same price point, using Volvo as an exemplar made it explicit that Subaru's frame of reference was "safe car." Thus, an exemplar can offer a precise way to represent the goal achieved by a brand. The positioning triangle for an exemplar frame of reference is shown in the top half of figure 5.4.

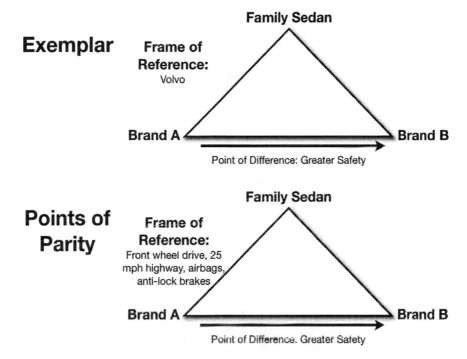

Figure 5.4: The Positioning Triangle for an exemplar and point of parity frames of reference

Points of Parity. Precision in communicating the frame of reference can also be achieved by using points of parity, which are characteristics shared by the alternatives that achieve a particular goal. For example, telling consumers that Volvo has front wheel drive, gets about 25 mph on the highway, has airbags and anti-lock brakes, describes in detail the goal that might be achieved if a Volvo were purchased. The positioning triangle for points of parity is shown in the bottom half of figure 5.4.

Using the Frame of Reference to Design Competitive Advertising Strategy

The primary role of a frame of reference is to inform consumers about the goal that can be achieved by using the advertised brand. But a frame of reference can also be used to help in distinguishing the brand from its competition. We examine three strategies that are useful for this purpose.

Making a Point of Difference a Point of Parity. One frame of reference strategy is to alert consumers to the fact that your brand possesses the competitors' point of difference, in effect making it a point of parity. As a result, this strategy elevates your points of difference and minimizes the reasons consumers have to buy the competitors' brand. For example, in the cleaning category Clorox is promoted as a powerful cleaner, whereas Oxi Clean is seen as safer for the environment. Clorox developed advertising that showed this brand being used to clean the toilet bowl, but at the same time it was safe enough that the family dog could drink out of the bowl without being harmed. The intent of this advertising was to make Oxi Clean's safety point of difference a point of parity, thus making Clorox's cleaning power the only point of product differentiation between the brands.

During those times when category demand is not growing, substantial use is made of this approach in an effort to steal share from competitors, which might be the only viable means of growth. Caution is needed when using this strategy to ensure that in the process of communicating that a competitors' point of difference is a point of parity, the brand's own point of difference remains clear. In addition, it is important that competitors are not in a position to turn the brand's point of difference into a point of parity.

Making a Frame a Point of Difference. A brand can sometimes affiliate itself with another category, and by doing so make that frame of reference the brand's point of difference. For example, Coffee Mate promotes its superior taste by comparing itself to cream. Consumers understand that Coffee Mate's frame of reference is a non-dairy creamer, but comparing itself to cream underscores Coffee Mate's taste superiority. Along similar lines, *Sports Illustrated* changed its frame from sports magazine to weekly news magazine and substantially increased its sales. Consumers' recognition that *Sports Illustrated* offered sports news did not change, but by comparing it against regular newspapers, the value of having the latest information become more apparent.

Reframing. In most cases, once a frame of reference is established, it is difficult to change. As we noted earlier, for many years Volvo promoted itself as a safe car. Attempts to change its frame of reference to a performance car were resisted by consumers. Similarly, Dash detergent, which was for many years positioned as a low sudsing detergent, failed in its attempt to reposition the brand when the demand for front-loading washers and therefore low sudsing detergents diminished, even though it was a superior cleaning product. The conclusion is that once a brand gains traction with consumers, its frame of reference (and thus its position) should not be changed. There is, however, at least one clear exception to this observation. It occurs when the brand is the first entrant in a category. Because a brand is a first entrant, its frame of reference is often another category. When a second competitor enters, a new category is typically established, which is adopted as the frame of reference. For example, as the first electronic calendar, Palm used paper calendars as the frame of reference to which it was superior in convenience. However, when other electronic calendars were introduced, the personal digital assistant category (PDA) was established. Palm was required to change the frame of reference from paper calendar to PDA. This reframing to PDA made convenience, which was Palm's point of difference in relation to paper calendars, a point of parity versus other PDAs. Thus, Palm was obligated to find new points of difference to be competitive with other PDAs.

Points of Difference

A brand's point of difference is a key element in positioning. The point of difference should be a benefit that not only sets the brand apart from competition, but also is perceived by consumers as a compelling reason to use the category. We examine three commonly used points of difference in positioning and advertising a brand: attributes, image and emotion. In this chapter we also discuss strategies that might be effective when promoting a parity brand, that is, a brand where no point of difference relative to the competition is evident.

Attributes

In most categories, attribute points of difference serve as the most powerful means of promoting rapid brand growth. Attributes can take the form of ingredients (Jif has more fresh roasted peanuts), country of origin (Dewar's Scotch is made in Scotland), and brand heritage (Bud is the king of beers).

Leading brands typically feature the benefit that drives category demand. Tide promotes superior cleaning and Budweiser features its superior taste. Brand leaders maintain their position even when features which they claim superiority are no better than those of competitors. Here, the point of difference is a greater expenditure against marketing than competitors. The second leading brand in a category typically selects a niche, and the third brand promotes its lower price. Jif, the leading brand of peanut butter promotes its superior taste; Skippy, the second leading brand, promotes its nutritional value, and Peter Pan, the third leading brand, promotes its lower price.

Despite the power of attributes in these various forms, their use as points of difference is often not sustainable. The reason is that for most brands unique features are easily imitable. Motorola's RAZR, which was introduced in 2004, experienced huge share growth for three years because of its stylish appearance and enhanced functionality. But when competitors first emulated these features and then surpassed them, RAZR's market share dropped from 20% to about 8% within a year. Thus, while potentially viable in the short-term, unless there is a barrier to competitive entry, brands often prefer to compete on some basis other than attributes because they are easier to sustain in the long run.

Image

When there are no barriers to competitive emulation, an image point of difference is often selected as the point of difference. Image focuses on who uses the brand and in what context. The product and its features might be presented, but who uses the product and in what context are focal. For example, IKEA promotes its furniture by showing the types of people who find its products attractive and by representing the contexts in which those people would view IKEA as a means of improving their environment. The products IKEA offers are shown in its advertising, but their features are not discussed. Office Depot is affiliated with NASCAR to highlight the types of people that patronize its stores. Nike employs professional athletes as a means of providing assurance for their superior performance point of difference. And fragrance brands typically employ celebrities to promote their brands because consumers are interested in the consequences of using a brand rather than its ingredients. Thus, Britney Spears, Paris Hilton, Paula Abdul, Derek Jeter and Shrck have all been affiliated with fragrance brands.

Image and attribute points of difference are sometimes featured in a complementary manner in advertising. Apple's "Get a Mac," campaign featured actors Justin Long as "Mac" and John Hodgman as "PC." They personify the computer systems they represent; Mac is young, friendly and confident, sporting a comfortable and casual look, whereas "PC" is an uptight, insecure, socially inept individual in drab, ill-fitting clothing. During their conversation, they discuss a feature on which Mac dominated PC such as making movies. In the three months following the launch of this campaign, Mac sales rose 12%. Microsoft launched a counterattack using spots featuring Bill Gates and Jerry Seinfeld as well as other personalities, but this response was met with Mac vs. PC spots that sustained the Get a Mac campaign by making fun of VISTA and other PC features. And despite the decline in computer sales as the recession set in, MAC's decline during 2009 was significantly smaller (8%) than that for PC (12%).

Emotion

Another approach to developing a point of difference is to show the emotional benefits derived from using the brand. These presentations resonate with current users if they capture their experience with the brand and draw attention from nonusers by having them experience the benefit. For example, Walt Disney World advertising shows the excitement kids experience in learning they are going to the theme park, and the fun the family has on the rides once they are there.

The disadvantage of image and emotion points of difference is that they are often not readily verifiable as functional differences to consumers, and thus require advertising to build and maintain. For example, it is easy for consumers to verify a feature such as "low calories," but the evidence that one will be hip, or elated by using the brand is often not as clear. In fact, often the reason to believe an image or emotion point of difference is due to the advertising for the brand. Croc shoes were cool and hip because the advertising conveyed this image. While it can be costly initially to build an image or emotional association, the advantage is that it is more difficult for the competition to respond. They cannot simply imitate a feature in the next generation of the product. Rather, they typically have to invest time and money in advertising.

Multiple Points of Difference: Brand Value

In most instances, effective communication of a position dictates that only a single point of difference be presented. This is because persuading people about a brand benefit usually requires substantial amplification. Presenting multiple benefits often results in none of the benefits being retained. Thus, when a new product is being introduced it is often necessary to inform consumers about its frame of reference and describe its point of difference in subsequent ads. Additional ads are also used to introduce new benefits. Using self-paced media such as newspapers, magazines and internet are good alternatives when it is important to present multiple features at the same time.

One situation where it is important to present multiple benefits is when the brand position pertains to value. Brand value is a function of two factors, the brand's quality and its cost. Quality can take two forms. It can refer to functional qualities of the product or to the emotional or psychological qualities experienced in using the product. Cost refers to the price of the product as well as the time required to use the product. Thus, value can be expressed in terms of an equation where value is enhanced when a brand's physical and psychological quality increase in relation to its cost in terms of money and time. The value equation can be represented as follows:

$$\textbf{Value} = \frac{\textbf{Quality (Functional + Psychological)}}{\textbf{Cost (Price + Time)}}$$

The value equation is conceptual in nature. Numbers cannot readily be plugged into the variables in the equation. Rather, brands compete by excelling at one or more elements of the value equation.

Historically, value was represented by quality in relation to price. More recently, time has been added to the equation because it has become a major cost in purchasing and using products. Between 1980 and 1990, the average American increased his or her work hours from 40 to 48 and reduced leisure time from 21 to 16 hours. With downsizing in the 1990s, the average worker added about another 45 minutes per day or one additional month per year of work time. And in the 2000s people reported greater fractionation of their leisure time: they had fewer large blocks of discretionary time. The consequence is that many people now experience *time famine*, or lack of time to accomplish the tasks they feel need to be managed. The result is that time has become an increasingly important factor in customers' assessments of value.

Consumers' predominant strategy to cope with time famine is multi-tasking. This typically involves accomplishing a goal while engaging in some obligatory activity. People make phone calls while driving in their cars, they eat while driving, and they exercise while walking to work. There has also been an adjustment in the choices consumers make. The population of dogs in this country is 72 million, which represents a 6% rate of growth in the past decade, while the population of cats is 82 million, which is a 12% increase in the past 10 years. In part, these trends reflect the fact that cats require less time to tend than do dogs. The purchase of nutritional pet foods such as *Science Diet* has grown dramatically, in part reflecting consumers' efforts to reduce the incidence of a pet's digestive distress that might require time-consuming visits to the veterinarian. Purchases of push lawn mowers have increased substantially in the U.S., which not only reflects an increased interest in green solutions, but also results from the fact that these devices enable the user to exercise while accomplishing the grass-cutting chore.

Several strategies emerge from using value as the point of difference. Brands such as McDonald's compete on all elements of the value equation. McDonald's offers good quality foods accompanied by fast service and a low price, which has the psychological benefit of making the consumer feel he or she is a smart shopper. Other brands use a value position by offering the same quality as competitive offerings, but at a lower price. This strategy, with its focus on the denominator of the value equation, is followed by brands such as Suave shampoo and Wal-Mart. Or a brand might compete in the numerator of the value equation by offering superior quality in the products and the experience of using it. Apple computer, iPhone, and Williams Sonoma apply this strategy.

No Points of Difference: Owning Category Essence

In a substantial number of cases, brands do not have a point of difference in relation to competition. Most airlines offer similar services and amenities, most telephones offer similar features, and most hotels at the same price point have similar rooms, restaurants, and lobbies. In these instances, consumer insight about the category is often used to differentiate a brand. For this reason, such a point of difference strategy is referred to as *category essence.* In using a category essence strategy, the assumption is that if a brand demonstrates an understanding of consumers' problems, it is the solution. For example, Lee Jeans promoted the brand by showing the problems women encountered in trying to fit into jeans. They were urged to buy Lee Jeans as a remedy to this problem. No reason was offered about why Lee would be superior to other brands in fit and there was no evidence they fit better. Nevertheless, the campaign was successful in stimulating purchase. Consumers inferred that because Lee understands their problem, they are likely to have developed a solution to it. In applying category essence, Lee Jeans' strategy was to undermine consumers' belief that competitors deliver points of parity, that is, what is expected of all brands in the category. Because Lee delivers these benefits, it would be viewed as superior.

The use of category essence is a viable way to distinguish a brand that otherwise has no point of difference from its competitors. However, it is often a strategy of last resort. Competitors typically have access to the same consumer insight and thus could emulate a category essence strategy. And as brands become less distinguishable over time, and more brands use category essence focusing on consumer insight, linkage of the insight to the brand is likely to become increasingly difficult to achieve.

Summary of Points of Difference Strategies

There are a variety of considerations when selecting an appropriate point of difference strategy. The main approaches discussed are summarized in table 5.1.

	Attribute	Image	Emotion	Category Essence
Focus	Product features	Who or what is associated with the product	Experience in using the product	Demonstrating understanding of consumer challenges with the category
Most effective when	• Rapid brand growth • Products with high barriers to entry	• Points of difference are imitable • Features not relevant	• Feeling when using the product is critical to purchase	• Little to no product differentiation in the category • Last resort
Example	iPhone (unique functionality highlighted)	The Gap (featuring laid back models in casual settings)	Herbal Essences (focus is on the experience of using the products)	Marriott Courtyard (knows business travelers)

Table 5.1: Points of Difference Strategies

Orchestrating the Selection of Attributes and Benefits

When developing a position, it is important to consider how the attributes and benefits used to specify the frame of reference and points of difference are related to each other. When they are positively correlated (e.g., smaller cars are associated with greater gas efficiency) consumers readily accept that the brand has these features. However, when brand features or benefits are negatively correlated (e.g., great performance and safety), consumers' are more difficult to convince. For example, several years ago Volvo attempted to compete with Lexus, BMW and Mercedes on performance and finished last. Consumers did not believe Volvo's performance claim because it is negatively correlated with Volvo's heritage of safety. If Volvo was safe, as it had claimed for many years, it could not also achieve high performance. Along the same lines, a claim that a product is low in calories often undermines the claim of good taste, and promoting a brand as inexpensive undermines a high quality claim.

One way to deal with the problem posed by such *negatively correlated attributes and benefits* is to explain to consumers that the benefits are, in fact, positively correlated. BMW, which was initially known for performance, introduced safety as an additional factor. As was suggested by Volvo's experience, performance and safety appear to be negatively correlated benefits that would prompt skepticism among consumers with respect to possessing both of these benefits. However, BMW represented safety as superior ability with respect to stopping and turning, which in effect presented both benefits as pertaining to performance. This strategic positioning led to the formulation of BMW as "The Ultimate Driving Machine." When Ford purchased Volvo, they attempted to follow this approach with the slogan "protect your body, ignite your soul," by making safety the basis for enjoying performance. Thus, the strategy rests on finding a plausible means of making benefits that seem to be negatively correlated appear to be positively related.

Brand Personality

Consumers often anthropomorphize brands. The recognition of this practice has prompted strategists to represent their brands as having a personality. This often involves adopting an Archetype for the brand. Archetypes were initially developed by psychiatrist Carl Jung in his research on cultural mythologies. Variants of Jung's archetypes have been used to personify brands. Twelve archetypes are common, though there are variants in the labeling of these archetypes. These are described below.

The **Magician** archetype is used by brands that promote transformative power and charisma. The Magician brand represents one that understands and uses the knowledge of the laws of nature to fulfill dreams. Apple's development of cutting edge technology such as the iPad and iPhone offers a good example of a Magician archetype.

The **Outlaw** archetype is based on the premise that rules are made to be violated. Outlaw brands value freedom and rebellion. They appeal to customers who feel disaffected from society by representing the brand as a break with convention. Harley has cultivated an Outlaw image for its motorcycles, even though many of its owners are white collar workers.

The **Jester** archetype highlights the enjoyment provided by the brand. Doritos is a salty snack that presents the brand's main attribute, crunch, in a manner that highlights the fun of eating the product.

The **Lover** archetype is employed by brands that attempt to build intimacy with their users. Products whose goal is to make people feel good (cosmetics, luxury goods, chocolate, ice cream) choose this archetype. Haagen-Dazs highlights the hedonic value of the brand in their advertising.

Everyman/woman archetype fosters a communal feeling and presents the brand as down-to-earth and approachable. Southwest Airlines emphasizes this archetype by treating all customers alike and maintaining low prices.

The **Caregiver** archetype is employed by brands that are protective, or that have the goal of achieving public good. Allstate highlights how the brand protects its consumers in the product offering and advertising ("You're in good hands with All State)."

The **Ruler** archetype is adopted by brands that are associated with power, leadership and status. Ruler brands promise prosperity to their users. An example of this archetype is American Express users, whose importance is recognized by their use of the card.

The **Creator** archetype represents brands that attempt to convey that they are visionary, and help promote consumers' self-expression. LEGO empowers its users to build objects that express their vision.

The **Innocent** archetype typifies brands associated with morality and goodness. This archetype is often used for kids' brands such as Fisher-Price ("Play. Laugh. Grow.").

The **Sage** archetype is one that represents a brand as a mentor or having special expertise. Google, which offers extensive online search, is promoted in this manner.

The **Explorer** archetype emphasizes individuality. Starbucks has adopted this archetype by developing a unique product and retail experience.

The **Hero** archetype is reflected in brands that present a feeling of strength and competence. Marlboro is a brand engenders a feeling of ruggedness and success by its association with the American West.

Archetypes are metaphors that are intended to capture the essence of the brand. They elevate the analysis of consumers' motivations for product use from purely rationale factors to a more symbolic level. And archetypes provide a characterization of the brand that is useful in making a strategic assessment of whether promoting a specific feature fits with the brand's persona. For example, it would be inappropriate for Doritos, which is typically represented as a Jester in advertising, to present detailed information about the brand's ingredients, or for Quaker Oats, which is most readily categorized as a Caregiver, to develop humorous light-hearted appeals.

Although archetypes serve to discipline product development and advertising strategies by helping a brand adhere to its character, archetypal analysis typically has not offered deep psychological insight that is needed to associate a brand uniquely with a specific archetype. This may be less of a problem when a brand seems to fit primarily into one archetype. For example, Harley Davidson seems to be nicely aligned with the Outlaw archetype. However, this becomes more challenging for brands whose persona intersects with more than one archetype. For example, Apple is characterized as a Magician, but it also can be viewed as a Creator or an Outlaw. When this occurs the value of Archetypes becomes more limited in offering strategic guidance. The study of brand archetypes is a fruitful direction for both academic and practitioner research efforts.

Evaluating a Brand Position

The adequacy of a brand position can be evaluated against four criteria. First, does the brand offer benefits that are desired by consumers? These benefits might take the form of attributes, image, emotion or category essence. If they do, the next question is whether the position can be owned? Addressing this question requires a consideration of whether the brand has a point of difference given the frame of reference with which it is associated. Third, it is important to determine whether the brand's position is navigable. Can it be steered in a manner so that the brand delivers on its promise? The most efficient way to kill a brand is to adopt a position that it cannot deliver. And finally, is the brand's position likely to endure over time? Good performance on these four criteria --desired by customers, owned and navigable as well as enduring--would suggest the position is DONE right (see figure 5.5)!

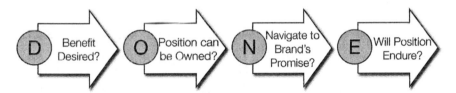

Figure 5.5: Evaluating a Brand Position

To illustrate, consider Guitar Hero, which offers consumers the opportunity to feel like they are playing guitar without having to devote the time required to master the instrument, a benefit that is *desired*. It would appear that Guitar Hero *owns* this benefit, because the only other alternative would seem to be air guitar, which does not deliver the same experience. The combination of a guitar that requires some dexterity to operate and the music videos that accompany it, suggest that Guitar Hero's position is *navigable*—it delivers the promised benefit. And with an ever growing repertoire of music and the availability of a new point of entry target every several years, the brand is expected to have *endurance* over time. Of course, when Rock Band entered the market the viability of this position needed to be reconsidered.

Summary of Brand Positioning: FOR & POD

Positioning involves developing a frame of reference and a point of difference. The frame of reference signals the purpose or goal of using the brand. It can be represented by a category, an exemplar, points of parity or by a statement of the goal itself. A frame of reference:

- Guides the selection of points of difference (and reverse).
- Suggests opportunities to grow your brand by attracting demand from other categories.
- Reduces likelihood of being blindsided by competitors who are achieving the same customer goal as your brand, but who hold membership in a different category.
- Can be developed by making competitors points of difference, points of parity.
- Can serve as a point of difference.

Points of difference can take the form of attributes, image, or emotion. Although attributes typically are most effective in stimulating demand they are often readily imitable. As a consequence, brands often turn to image points of difference. Emotional points of difference are powerful when brand consumption is affectively based. When a brand is at parity with competitors, consumer insight or superior budget can be used to distinguish a brand from its competitors.

Chapter Exercises

- Practice writing a position statement for a brand. The brand might be one of your choosing or you can consider one of the following well-known brands: Snickers, BMW, Kellogg Graduate School of Management. The template that follows may be used to write the positioning statement:
  For _____ (target), this brand is the _____ (frame of reference) that offers _____ (points of difference) because _____ (reason to believe). This brand is also _____ (brand personality).

- Pick a brand that you like. How could the brand gain leverage over the competition via the value equation discussed in the chapter. Are there multiple routes by which the brand can dominate the competition? What are the advantages and disadvantages for the brand with respect to different aspects of the value equation?

- Use the DONE framework to evaluate the current positioning of an existing brand. In doing so, also consider the chosen point of difference. Is the point of difference an attribute, image, emotion, or category essence? Do you think the chosen point of difference is the best choice for the brand relative to the competition?

Recommended Reading

Kevin Keller, Brian Sternthal, and Alice M. Tybout (2002), "Three Questions You Need to Ask About Your Brand," *Harvard Business Review*, pp. 80-89.

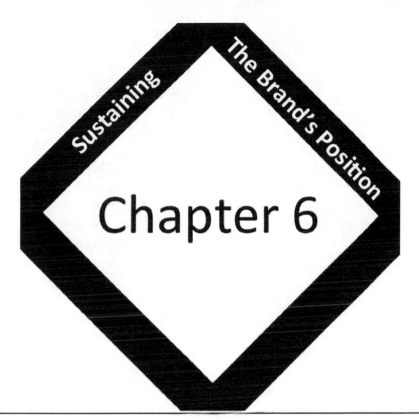

Sustaining The Brand's Position

Chapter 6

Chapter 6 Objectives

- Explore strategies for and the benefits of sustaining brand positioning
    - o Maintaining the same positioning
    - o Enriching the current positioning
- Considerations for repositioning

Reebok emerged as a major athletic shoe brand in the mid-1980s. Brand development was based on the insight that women were exercising in substantial numbers. Reebok's position stated that women could enhance their performance when exercising by wearing a shoe that provided exceptional comfort and fit. This claim was supported by the development of shoes made from garment quality leather. When research indicated that the vast majority of people wearing athletic shoes never ventured onto a court or used the shoes to engage in other athletic activities, Reebok aired advertising that showed people wearing Reeboks to do non-athletic activities such as walking and picnicking.

In response to this campaign, Reebok surpassed Nike as the leading athletic shoe in the US in 1987. Many consumers were purchasing Reeboks as a casual shoe. Within two years, however, consumer preferences changed. Off-court use of running shoes was replaced by brown shoes. Reebok's share dropped from 33% to 18 % of the market. Reebok was perceived as a woman's casual shoe that was comfortable because it was made with garment leather. Efforts were then made to promote Reebok as a performance shoe because use of the shoes for athletic activities was driving category sales. Reebok supported a performance position by developing the PUMP, which allowed the Reebok wearer to vary the air pressure in the shoe and thus get a snug fit, by introducing the first cross-training shoe, and by using celebrity athletes to promote the brand. None of these initiatives was successful in positioning Reebok as a performance shoe.

Reebok's brand history offers a sharp contrast with the history of Nike. Whereas Nike initially developed and sustained its position as a performance brand, Reebok gained traction as a women's shoe that was for casual use rather than high performance. Attempts to reposition the brand as a performance shoe met with limited success. This history underscores the more general finding that once a brand position is developed and becomes familiar to consumers, it is difficult and costly to change. This observation implies that strategies for sustaining a position are critical to viable long-term brand performance.

In this chapter, we examine advertising strategies to sustain a brand's position. These strategies include maintaining the same strategy and execution over time, maintaining the brand's position by presenting it to the consumer in a contemporary manner, and enriching the brand's position either by introducing additional reasons to believe the brand's position or by using functional benefits to infer emotional ones. We also assess the benefits of sustaining a brand position and the challenges of changing a position.

Strategies for Sustaining a Position

Can you name a brand with a well established market position that was repositioned successfully? There are very few. Why is this case? One reason is that once a positioning is encoded in consumers' long-term memory, time is required for people to forget the old positioning and learn the new one. Thus, the preferred strategy is to adopt a position that sustains a brand's long-term viability. We review several position-sustaining strategies that depend primarily on advertising to help a brand maintain its current position over time.

Maintaining the Same Position and Execution

One strategy for sustaining a position involves maintaining the same position and creative execution over time. This is the strategy followed by Marlboro. Since the 1950s, Marlboro has been promoted as the masculine cigarette brand. In the U.S., advertising features cowboys who exhibit a goal-directed and self-assured demeanor, and in South America masculinity has been symbolized by using Formula One race cars as the icon for masculinity. This strategy has been successful because the instantiations that imply masculinity have not changed over time.

Maintaining the Same Position but Changing the Execution

For most brands it is not possible to follow the positioning strategy that has been so successful for Marlboro. Rather, the challenge is to maintain the same position over time and to make the instances in which the position is presented contemporary. For example, from the time of its launch, Nike has been positioned as the brand for those who aspire to peak athletic performance. However, the personification of this benefit has changed over time to represent contemporary athletes and athletic endeavors. Similarly, Betty Crocker, which produced a variety of baked goods, used a fictitious woman as the icon to represent the modern homemaker who relies on Betty Crocker mixes to produce superior baked goods. Over time, eight different images were used to represent Betty Crocker; at times she was younger or older, professional or a homemaker, and multicultural or not. The choice of icon depended on how women's roles were perceived in the culture at that time. But despite these executional changes, Betty Crocker's position as a producer of quality baked goods did not change. We refer to this strategy as *modern instantiation of a position.*

Another approach to modern instantiation is to update the iconography presented on the package. For example, Pepsi has changed its package design to make the brand more contemporary. The presentation of the brand name vertically rather than horizontally was adopted for this purpose. This change might be perceived by consumers as contemporary because it bears a resemblance to the Obama logo that was used in the 2008 presidential campaign: both use red, white and blue, both have circles and stripes.

Modern instantiation of a position can also be achieved by the association of the brand's benefit with contemporary values. Along these lines, Special K is positioned as a nutritional cereal that was part of a diet that had the benefit of helping women maintain a slim figure. More recently, the nutritional benefit has been associated with being physically fit rather than being slim, which is in keeping with motivations expressed by contemporary women for consuming nutritional products.

Enriching the Position

In some situations, it is necessary to enrich consumers' knowledge with additional brand news in order to sustain the brand's position. For example, consider the positioning of Pantene, a shampoo marketed by P&G. The brand's target is women 25-54 who are concerned with their appearance and aspire to achieve beauty. Pantene's functional benefit is that regular use will make hair healthy: shiny, smooth and strong. The reason to believe this benefit is that Pantene contains a special ingredient or attribute, its Pro V vitamin formula. In addition, because Pantene makes hair healthy, the product delivers an emotional benefit: it enhances the users' confidence that they look attractive, which prompts them to be more outgoing, which results in better relationships, thereby making them feel good about themselves. By analogy, these inferences are like rungs of a ladder, where the consumer need that is being met by a brand progresses from physical and functional to social and self-actualizing as the ladder is ascended. Thus, the implication of each rung serves as the next rung of the ladder. We refer to the inferential process to enrich knowledge of a brand's position as laddering.

In most cases, a brand's position is initially presented in terms of the functional benefit it offers consumers. This is because in most situations consumers begin by evaluating their goals in terms of a functional benefit; they want products that are economical, convenient, efficient, and healthy. Thus, the point of entry to the ladder is at the functional level. To persuade consumers about a brand's functional benefit a reason to believe is presented. This reason to believe typically is an attribute or a typical or well-known user of the product. We refer to this process as *laddering down*. Following the same logic, the implication of the functional benefit in terms of an emotional benefit is referred to as *laddering up* (see figure 6.1). We examine strategies for laddering down and laddering up.

Laddering Down. Providing support for a functional benefit with an attribute or reason to believe involves laddering down. This reason often takes the form of an attribute or ingredient. For example, Colgate Total toothpaste is positioned as offering superior dental hygiene. It uses its Triciosan ingredient to support the benefit claim of superior protection against gingivitis. Triciosan represents Colgate's reason to believe just as the Pro V ingredient formulation does for Pantene. For fragrances, the reason to believe a benefit (i.e., a desirable smell) might be the endorsement of the celebrity (e.g., Paris Hilton, Nicole Kidman).

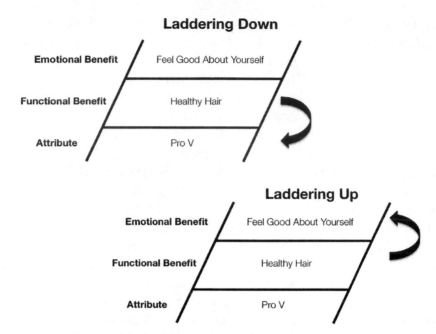

Figure 6.1: Laddering Up versus Laddering Down

Laddering down can serve to sustain a brand when the functional benefit is supported by multiple attributes. Along these lines, United Airlines can be positioned as the most convenient airline and this functional benefit can be sustained by introducing multiple attributes over time. The destinations to which United travels, its curbside check-in, and its online boarding pass service can all be used as reasons to believe the convenience benefit. Each of these attributes adds news and reminds people of earlier promoted reasons to believe because all of the reasons are associated with convenience. This use of multiple attributes sustains a brand position by continually providing news to support the belief that the brand provides a specific functional benefit. And by keeping the functional benefit (and other icons) the same across ads enhances the likelihood that people will link the brand and the benefit. The introduction of multiple attributes over time that imply the functional benefit was developed by the Leo Burnett ad agency and is referred to as the *Big Idea*.

Laddering Up. Laddering up entails first promoting an attribute, and then using this attribute as the basis for a functional benefit. In turn, the functional benefit serves as the basis for an emotional benefit. Consider how San Pellegrino sparkling water might apply a laddering up strategy for three targets with different motivations for category use: achievement-oriented, physical wellness-oriented, and self-esteem building. A physical feature of the brand is used to imply a functional benefit, which in turn implies an emotional benefit (figure 6.2).

Figure 6.2: San Pellegrino Laddering Up Across Different Targets
(Adapted from CoreInsights)

Doug Milliken of The Clorox Company has developed an alternative metaphor to the ladder to describe the relationship between attributes and more abstract benefits. His notion is that a bridge links consumers to the brand. This depiction is shown in figure 6.3. At one end of the bridge is the consumer, who is interested in fulfilling a goal through brand purchase. At the other end of the bridge is the brand, which is associated with attributes.

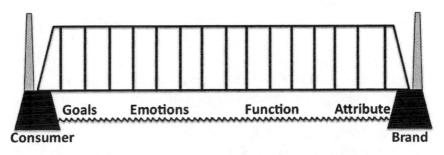

Figure 6.3: The Bridge Metaphor for Brand Positioning

There are four stations on the bridge:

Attribute: Why I believe this
Functional Benefit: What it does for me
Emotional Benefit: How this makes me feel
Goals: Why I care about this

Although the bridging metaphor includes the same inferential steps as the ladder, the bridge is instructive in highlighting the fact that when a position identifies product features (attributes) and functional benefits, the focus is on the brand. In contrast, a position developed in terms of emotional benefits focuses attention on how consumers situate a brand in their life space. The bridge also highlights the fact that consumers can be situated at a number of places on the bridge. One segment might only be interested in the functional benefit; men might only care that a shampoo cleans their hair. Another segment might be drawn by the emotional benefits of a brand. Here, it might be necessary to have the consumer cross the bridge by persuading them about the functional benefits and the attributes before promoting the emotional benefits.

Bridging or laddering up from attribute to a functional benefit to a more abstract emotional benefit provides a basis for informing consumers of a brand's essence or core value. This essence is often conveyed to consumers by relating the focal brand to disparate objects that prompt the same feeling as is experienced by using the brand. To convey Old Navy's essence as representing casual and unpretentious clothing, it is associated with objects that share this characteristic; those who hold clerical jobs, drive a Ford Focus or Honda Civic, go to movies, and eat at McDonald's. In contrast, Banana Republic's essence might be associated with those who hold managerial positions, drive a BMW or Lexus, go to the symphony and dine in establishments that are associated with multiple dollar signs in restaurant reviews.

Laddering or bridging can sometimes be achieved in a single ad, particularly if the medium used to transmit information is self-paced. In many situations, however, laddering and bridging require the development of multiple executions over time to capture different stages of the ladder or place on the bridge. To be effective, it is critical that there is strong linkage among the ads. Further, the success of a laddering campaign depends in part on consumers' recall of the previous advertising when seeing the current generation. It is important that consumers recall the product feature or attribute when the ad describes a functional benefit, and recall both the functional benefit and attribute when the ad presents an emotional benefit. In McDonald's advertising, a combination of repeating previous benefits, the iconography of the golden arches and use of the same jingle enhance the chances that consumers will connect the information in a current ad with that presented in earlier ads for McDonald's. Some ads might focus on supporting the functional benefit of tasty food by highlighting attributes such as ingredients or taste while others focus on illustrating how McDonald's can be a part of quality time with family or the convenience of its offerings. Alternatively, at each stage in the ladder, consumers can be reminded briefly of prior stages on which the current stage depends.

Sustaining a Position versus Repositioning

Sustaining a benefit over time often serves as a barrier to competitive entry. When a brand has maintained the same position and execution over a significant period of time, competitors cannot readily compete by emulating it unless the competitor is willing to spend heavily over an extended period of time. Energizer could not compete with Duracell on longevity, a position that Duracell had maintained for many years. American Tourister could not compete with Samsonite on durability, because Samsonite advertising had made durability synonymous with the brand. Reebok could not convince people that it was the performance shoe, because that was Nike's position from its inception. Thus, like product, price, and distribution strategies, advertising can serve as a barrier to competitive entry.

Sustaining a position is also beneficial because the alternative is repositioning, and most brand repositions fail. As we noted in **Chapter 5**, Dash was a highly effective detergent that failed in its effort to change the position from low sudser. Tab, the diet soft drink, attempted to reposition the brand so that it would not be perceived as being only for females by changing its packaging. This effort failed to attract men.

Although successful repositioning is unlikely for most brands, there are circumstances under which it might be achieved. Repositioning can be effective when few consumers are aware of the brand's original position. Marlboro cigarettes, which were initially positioned as a woman's cigarette, was successfully repositioned as a masculine cigarette because there were few consumers who were familiar with the brand. Lack of familiarity with a brand also occurs for established brands when the target is composed of consumers who are entering the category. Miller beer repositioned the brand by targeting point of entry consumers, who did not know of prior problems with the beer's quality because it had occurred prior to the time when they had an interest in the beer category. Repositioning is easier in such cases because brands do not need to overcome any negative associations consumers have with the brand from memory.

Repositioning can also be effective if the modification in the position is small. Thus, Aleve was successful in repositioning the brand from an analgesic (general pain relief) to a narrower position of arthritis pain relief.

Finally, as we noted in discussing reframing, repositioning is essential when a brand is a first entrant and a second entrant joins the category. When Palm entered the market as the first PDA, the frame of reference was paper calendars/manual organizers as PDA's were otherwise unknown and this group represented Palm's primary competition. Palm was positioned as a more convenient way to be organized. When new PDA competitors emerged, Palm's frame of reference was changed from a paper calendar to a PDA and Palm repositioned itself as the more efficient PDA that thinks ahead for you. The change in Palm's frame of reference necessitated by the entry of other brands required a change in its point of difference.

In the vast majority of situations, repositioning is not a viable strategy because it requires a significant amount of time and substantial resources. VW successfully repositioned Škoda from the lowest price car to a value car. But it took almost a decade for Škoda to become a viable brand and it required substantial expenditures to develop the production facility, different models, dealerships and the marketing support necessary to be a successful brand.

Summary of Developing and Sustaining a Position

The process of developing and sustaining a position is summarized in figure 6.4. The overall framework can be decomposed into three separate decision trees related to (1) Establishing the Frame of Reference, (2) Developing a Point of Difference, and (3) Sustaining Positioning. Within each of these trees there are particular strategies a brand might adopt to accomplish the goal.

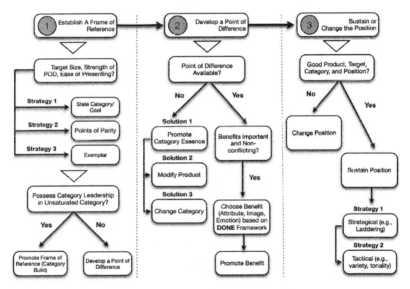

Figure 6.4: Summary of Positioning Strategies

The first decision tree involves establishing a frame of reference. In addressing this issue, a decision must be made about whether the frame of reference is other brands in the same category as the target brand, or whether it includes brands from disparate categories that can accomplish the same goal as the focal brand. Whatever the frame of reference, it can be made operational to consumers by highlighting its points of parity with other brands having the same frame of reference (strategy 1), by relating it to an exemplar for the category (strategy 2), or by simply announcing the goal that is accomplished by using the brand (strategy 3). When a brand has leadership in a category and the category is unsaturated, the positioning strategy might entail a category build, which would promote the category in which a brand holds membership over other categories. In effect, a category build is interpreted as a means of promoting the frame of reference. Category build can stand alone, or it can be done in conjunction with a brand build strategy, in which separate ads for each strategy are typically required.

When a frame of reference has been established, attention shifts to developing a point of difference. Leaders should consider the benefit that drives the category, and outshout competition on this benefit. Followers should consider adopting a niche, where they have a barrier to competitive entry. Of course, the first question one has to ask is whether there is a point of difference available. If not, it is important to understand why there is no point of difference. If it is because the category is one where all products are on parity (e.g., blank CD-roms), it might be possible to differentiate a brand by demonstrating that it understands consumers' problems (solution 1). By demonstrating that the brand understands the consumer, the brand can attract consumers from competitors. This category essence approach is a strategy of last resort because there are typically few barriers to competitive emulation. However, it is also possible that a lack of point of difference stems from an inferior product or one that is dominated by the competition on all important dimensions. In the latter case, advertising is not the likely solution for salvaging the brand. Rather, the brand should consider fixing the product and/or engage in product innovation (solution 2). Finally, if the product is not a problem a brand might also consider whether it could dominate in another category. For example, a tasty health snack might find itself competing better against desserts than health foods (solution 3).

When a point of difference is found for a brand, two questions are posed. First, does the brand have a benefit that is important to consumers? If the benefit is unimportant to consumers a new benefit must be found, or an effort might be made to educate consumers about the benefit's importance. Second, is the benefit negatively correlated with other benefits promoted by the brand? If the benefits are important and not negatively correlated, it can be a viable basis for a brand's position. If the benefits are unimportant or negatively corre-lated these problems must be resolved or the strategy rethought. Once these issues are resolved, the benefit can be promoted. In general, there is a preference for benefits based on attributes rather than image because consumers are typically more responsive to attribute-based positions. However, attribute differences in many categories are easi-er for competition to emulate than an image-based position. When barriers to competitive attribute emulation don't exist, image is the preferred basis for positioning.

When a point of difference has been found, it can be sustained using a variety of different strategies. The simplest is to sustain the same benefit and execution over time as Marlboro has done (strategy 1). In most cases, however, while the same benefit can be presented, a modern instantiation is needed if the brand is to be perceived as con-temporary (strategy 2). Another option is to ladder down by introduc-ing different attributes that imply the benefit over time to sustain news and maintain the brand's position (strategy 3). Finally, ladder-ing up from a functional to an emotional benefit can be undertaken when category and brand consumption is based on emotion (strategy 4).

Chapter Exercises

- Consider the strategies of laddering and bridging. Imagine you are a brand manager for a new organic frozen pizza (or another category if you prefer). How might you enter that market? Devel-op a long-term strategy by drawing a laddering or bridging strate-gy you would execute. Based on the ladder or bridging strategy you create, outline three different ad campaigns you would run to (a) educate the consumer on the benefit offered, (b) solidify the positioning by laddering down to reasons to believe, and (c) lad-der up to provide an emotional benefit to the consumer

- Think about a recent brand that you have seen attempting to repo-sition itself. Does the repositioning appear to be successful? Why or why not?

- Think about a brand that has been enduring over time. In your experience growing up with the brand, what strategies from the sustaining positioning figure were employed in order to maintain the brand over time? What elements of its positioning statement strategy facilitated the brand's long-term success?

Chapter 7

Chapter 7 Objectives

- Describe the characteristics of the media that present advertising
- Strategies for selecting advertising media
- Strategies for selecting advertising vehicles
- Strategies for dominance: matching, monopolizing, mindset, moment
- Developing an advertising budget

UPS handles over 60% of all ground parcel deliveries in the United States, which is considerably more than its two nearest rivals, Federal Express and the US Post Office. UPS is also second to Federal Express with a 34% share of the overnight air freight market (vs. 42%). UPS deliveries are supported by 2,400 distribution centers, 93,000 vehicles, and 268 airplanes that travel to 391 airports in the USA and 219 abroad. Over the last decade, UPS and the Martin Agency have attempted to grow the brand by advertising in two ways. One is to reinforce the fact that UPS offered extremely fast delivery services. For this purpose, UPS aired the "Race the Truck" campaign featuring NASCAR legend Dale Jarrett. The other strategy was to make customers aware of its broad array of services including international shipping and small business services. Initially, UPS launched the "What Can Brown Do for You" campaign to identify its services. This was followed by the recent $35 million "Whiteboard" campaign, which provides a more in depth analysis of the solutions that UPS offers its customers.

The Whiteboard campaign employed several different media. TV spots featured spokesperson Andy Azula, who is a creative director at the Martin Agency. He used a whiteboard to illustrate the solution UPS provides to a common logistical problem. For example, in one spot he described pictorially how UPS could enhance supply chain efficiency, and in another how UPS services facilitated international shipping (www.youtube.com/watch?v=95EeUAvAba4). The spots invited people to the UPS microsite, which provided the opportunity to explore solutions interactively that pertained specifically to their business (http://whiteboard.ups.com). UPS also hosted a website (www.upsalamode.com) that documented how UPS served the fashion industry by offering timely and fast shipment of materials and finished product to their destinations. This website reported case studies of how UPS served the fashion industry and featured the winner of the UPS fashion contest. In addition, radio and billboards were used to reinforce UPS' position and prompt people to go to the website. Direct mail emphasizing the whiteboard theme and offering incentives to use UPS were sent to small and medium size businesses.

As a foundation for strategic analysis, **Chapter 7** describes the characteristics of the major media in which advertising is placed.

Once this foundation has been laid, **Chapter 8** continues with a discussion of the planning and assessment of media strategy.

The Media

Expenditures in advertising media for 2008 and 2009 are shown in table 7.1. The total expenditure on media advertising in the United States for 2008 was about $270.8 billion, which is a 3.2 % decrease in relation to 2007 spending—not surprising given the recession. The forecasted expenditure for 2009 advertising was a 7.6% lower than it was in 2008. With the exception of Internet, cable, and syndication TV, all media were expected to lose ad revenues in 2009. Newspapers and TV have been hardest hit. On a worldwide basis, the spending on advertising has grown from $474 billion in 2000 to approximately $641 billion in 2009. We begin our analysis of media strategy by describing the key characteristics of major media. This analysis of the strengths and limitations of each medium provides a basis for judging the appropriateness of a medium given a particular marketplace scenario.

The media listed in table 7.1 can be classified in three categories: Static, dynamic and interactive. UPS's advertising history illustrates the strategic use of each of these types of media. Static media provide advertising information all at once. In the UPS case, the static media included direct marketing and billboards. Direct marketing provides detailed information about UPS that is relevant to a specific target. Billboards remind people about UPS functions that were learned about elsewhere and serves as a prompt to visit the website for more information. TV and radio are dynamic media. TV provides an opportunity to illustrate the problem solution UPS offers to a large audience. Radio offers a way to deliver a frequent reminder about the brand. The UPS website is an interactive medium (i.e., it requires engagement by the consumer); although the number of people exposed to the website is likely to be a small percent of the TV audience for UPS's advertising, those visiting the website can access applications that are most relevant to them and interact with the advertiser to gain further knowledge. Thus, static, dynamic and interactive media each serve distinct purposes. We examine the properties of each medium in detail.

Medium	2008		2009 Forecast	
	In millions of dollars	Share	In millions of dollars	Share
National				
Four TV Networks	17.2	6.4	15.9	6.2
National Spot TV	9.8	3.6	8.8	3.4
Cable Network TV	21.4	7.9	21.7	8.4
Broadcast Syndication TV	3.6	1.3	3.6	1.4
National Radio	3.8	1.4	3.6	1.4
Magazines	12.9	4.7	12.1	4.7
National Newspaper	5.9	2.2	5.4	2.1
Direct Mail	59.6	22	58.4	22.6
Yellow Pages	2.3	.8	2.1	1.1
Internet	11.4	4.1	11.9	4.6
Other National Media	37.1	13.7	36.1	14.0
Total National Media	**185.1**		**179.5**	
Local				
Local Newspapers	29.8	11.0	26.3	10.1
Local TV	13.1	4.8	12.2	4.7
Local Radio	13.7	5.1	12.9	5.0
Local Yellow Pages	11.7	4.3	11.1	4.3
Other Local Media	17.4	6.4	16.7	6.5
Total Local Media	**85.7**		**79.2**	
Grand Total	**270.8**		**258.7**	

Table 7.1: Media Expenditures for 2008-2009

Static Media

Magazines. Magazines can be classified into three major categories: consumer, business, and farm. In 2009, there were about 7,200 consumer magazines, of which only a third have significant circulation. Some of these are general interest magazines, such as *People* and *Time*. Others are segmented in terms of geography, demography or some other variable. For example, *Seventeen* appeals to teens, *Car and Driver* to automotive buffs, and *Essence* to African American readers. To compete with these special interest publications, general interest magazines typically offer a variety of editions. *Time*, for example, offers many different editions, including editions that deliver relevant information specifically to corporate executives and one for primary school students (Time for Kids).

Business publications are targeted at members of the business community. Some publications, such as *Ohio Tavern News* are aimed at particular industries (www.ohiotavernnews.com). Others attempt to attract business people who perform a particular function. For example, *Purchasing.com* is a publication that reaches purchasing agents in different industries. In all, there are several thousand business publications with combined circulation of about 60 million.

Business magazine advertising is efficient because there is little waste circulation on non-prospects and because unit cost is low (typically between $2,000 and $5,000 per page). Moreover, in many business publications, the purchase of space provides the advertiser with the leverage necessary to get publicity in the editorial sections of the magazine. Despite these attractive features of business publications, there is some discontent with them because reliable data about the audience for various books is not always available. Choice of business publications is often based on circulation and intuitions about reader characteristics rather that data about audience size and characteristics.

Farm publications deal primarily with the business side of farming. However, some farm publications also address issues related to farm life. Thus, these publications attract advertisers who wish to promote products and services used in farming as well as those used in other facets of farm life. Farm publications tend to be regional in nature and selective in terms of the type of farming they focus on (e.g., dairy vs. grape farming).

Magazines offer the advertiser several advantages. They are typically highly selective, thus allowing the advertiser to reach the target efficiently. Magazines allow the use of long copy and have exceptional catalog value (i.e., consumers can easily look back at the ad or spend additional time on the ad). Color reproduction of illustrations is also excellent. Technology allows late closing dates. In turn, this enables advertisers to maintain the currency of the information included in magazine ads.

On the downside, magazines often have a high level of clutter. For example, a substantial amount of space in general interest magazines is devoted to advertising products such as liquor, automobiles, and cigarettes, though ad spending in this latter category has dropped significantly in the past several years. A substantial percentage of the readership is achieved by pass-along, that is, readership by people other than those purchasing the magazine. The result is that the audience accumulates slowly, which is a problem when demand must be stimulated in a narrow time window. For example, about half the barbecue sauce in the U.S. is consumed around the Memorial Day, July 4th and Labor Day holidays. Advertising that is placed early enough in the season so that both the primary readers and pass-along readers see it, runs the risk that initial readers will have forgotten the ad by the time the use occasion comes around. If the ad is placed in closer proximity to the event, there is the possibility that the pass-along audience will see the ad too late for it to be relevant. When such timeliness is needed, broadcast media are appropriate because they accumulate whatever audience they will attain at the time of airing.

Although the number of magazines continues to grow, overall readership has not. As a result, more emphasis has been given to *custom published* magazines to reach consumers. For example, Saks Fifth Avenue distributes a publication called 5 to its best customers. And Lexus has both a hard copy and online publication for its customers and other interested parties. These publications provide information about a firm's brands along with entertainment and newsworthy information.

Newspapers. There are some 1,200 daily newspapers, 800 Sunday papers, and about 6,500 weeklies. Daily newspapers are read routinely in about 54% of American homes during the week, and 62% of homes on Sundays. Circulation of daily newspapers is currently about 53 million, in a steady decline from a high of 62.5 million in 1993.

Newspapers provide advertisers with a means of reaching the vast majority of consumers with timely information. Newspapers are flexible, enabling the advertiser to tailor the message to each community. They also enable the transmission of detailed information because the medium is self-paced. And they provide an attractive medium for retail advertising where a quick consumer response is often desired. Nevertheless, some advertisers are reluctant to use newspapers because they are not selective demographically, photographic reproduction is inconsistent, and advertising does not stand out in the clutter.

The Internet poses a substantial threat to newspapers as they currently operate. This is not because large numbers of people will switch from reading newspapers to some online equivalent. The risk occurs because of local newspapers' business model. On average, want ads provide about sixty percent of a newspaper's revenue. Such services are readily produced online by sources such as Craigslist. Although major newspapers are now developing these services, online want ads are priced significantly lower than off-line ads, thus severely reducing newspaper revenues. The reduction in advertising revenues has reduced the coverage provided by newspapers, which in turn has fueled the decline in their circulation.

Outdoor, Signage and Transit. Outdoor advertising takes several forms, but it most typically refers to billboards. An outdoor location allows the advertiser to reach a broad spectrum of the population and to register its brand name and perhaps a slogan. Thus, it is particularly useful to remind consumers of well-known products. Billboards can be used in conjunction with other media to enhance the brand name recognition of new products. Billboards can also be strategically selected to target a narrow segment (e.g., people taking a particular route to work), and to reach consumers at the moment they are thinking about the category (e.g., fast foods). However, it is hard to communicate substantial information with billboards.

Billboards have traditionally been a stationary form of advertising, but they can also be moving, as is the case of signage on trucks and buses. Billboards have traditionally been located outdoors, but they now appear indoors in the form of signage at sporting events and other venues where audiences congregate. With the rise in environmental concerns, the use of billboards has come under great criticism. This trend has limited the growth of this medium.

Transit advertising is presented on buses, rapid transit cars, in airline terminals, and the like. By judicious selection of the corridors in which transit advertising is placed, it can be made a highly selective medium. As is the case for outdoor, transit advertising is most appropriate to transmit brief messages. This limitation can be offset somewhat by "take-ones" which either provide the consumer with additional information or inform the consumer about where additional information can be found. Transit has grown dramatically during the last decade due to purchases made by packaged goods and services firms attempting to reach the buyers who are no longer reachable by daytime TV. Transit can also reach commuters who are traveling to shopping or other product consumption destinations.

Directories. Directories are books that list people, professions, institutions or the like. Perhaps the best-known advertising directory is the Yellow Pages, which are consulted by more than 75 percent of all adults in the United States. Consumers use this directory on average about 40 times a year. The Yellow Pages are used when consumers have identified a need, are in a purchasing mode and require information about where and what to buy. Yellow Pages are challenged by the availability of online search sites such as Craigslist and Google.

Dynamic Media

Television. Television advertising is delivered in several ways. Network involves beaming commercials from a single location to network affiliates across the country. The four networks in the United States account for less than 40% of the audience. This is a huge decline from the over 90% share of market enjoyed by the CBS, NBC and ABC in the mid-1980s. Thus, the ability to reach most of the population by airing advertising on a few channels has declined substantially as cable television has grown.

A second type of television advertising is termed spot and local. These are beamed from a particular television station to consumers in the viewing area. A distinction is made between spot and local to signify the type of advertiser. Manufacturers such as Procter & Gamble purchase spot advertising, whereas retailers such as Jewel Osco purchase local advertising. Spot rates are higher than local rates because the manufacturer typically uses an ad agency that is paid by the medium, whereas retailers often do not use an agency (at least that is the logic). Thus, retailers pay a rate that is equal to the manufacturers' spot rate minus the commission that would otherwise be paid to the ad agency. Manufacturers can take advantage of the lower local rates by engaging in cooperative advertising with retailers.

The decision of whether to use network or spot/local television advertising is based on the advertiser's objectives. If the advertiser distributes a product nationally and wishes to reach the entire population, network advertising is appropriate. Indeed, if the budget spent to achieve national coverage via network TV were placed in spot buys, only about 50 to 60 percent of the country could be covered. Spot/local advertising is useful when the advertiser is planning a regional rollout, has only sufficient resources to advertise in selected markets, or wishes to "heavy up" advertising either against regions of substantial brand sales or areas where there is an opportunity for brand growth.

A third type of television is cable. Cable has grown dramatically to become the leading television alternative during the past decade. It not only reaches over 60% of the US population, but it allows the advertiser to narrowcast. For example, ESPN, the leading cable station, reaches over 70% of cable viewers who are interested in sports. The Univision Network reaches about 83% of Hispanic households in the US.

A final type of television advertising involves syndication. Programs are created and sold to network affiliates, cable stations, independent stations and the like. *Seinfeld* and *Sex in the City* are examples of syndicated programming, which is based on the idea that people are loyal to shows, not stations. Syndication offers a way of achieving reach, especially during early fringe (4pm – 6pm) and prime access (7pm – 11pm) when network coverage is not available.

Television is an attractive medium for presenting advertising. It enables the advertiser to communicate with a substantial number of potential buyers quickly and often. The multi-sensory aspect of television is another attractive feature. It facilitates the portrayal of action and emotion as well as the demonstration of product features. At the same time, television has several limitations. It does not have catalog value; the audience often cannot refer back to the commun-ication, except as it is represented in memory. The large number of commercials shown on television also adversely affects advertising recall. A study conducted by TNS Media Intelligence indicated that prime time network television contained 14 minutes and 17 seconds of ad messages per hour and another 8 minutes and 15 seconds of brand appearances within programs. Late night TV has even more of both types of brand presentations. Thus, a firm's commercial may be competing with a dozen or more other commercials presented in the same hour and three or more commercials at any one interruption.

To pack more commercials into an already substantial amount of advertising time per hour, advertisers shortened the average ad time. Twenty years ago, 15 second spots represented 40% of all ads. This strategy adversely affected consumer recall as the consumers' exposure per ad was decreased and the clutter from competing ads was increased. The trend has reversed and today 15 second ads represent approximately 15% of commercials as advertisers have increased their use of longer formats. One such format is info-mercials. These are typically hour long advocacies for a brand. Health and cooking related products have made particularly effective use of infomercials. Another format involves the development of programs that are entertaining and informative. Although the sponsoring brand does not advertise during the program, information is included about the sponsoring brand. Tropicana developed a program that informed consumers about healthful consumption alternatives and included some recipes that had Tropicana as an ingredient. Finally, Hulu addresses clutter by streaming shows from various networks on the Internet. Hulu is not ad free, but it airs only a few commercials, and the viewer sometimes receives a choice of which ad from several listed they wish to view.

The growth of cable TV has made the television medium a less attractive means of achieving broad reach of the population. As noted earlier, networks reach less than 40% of the population. Because the audience is fractionated among the networks and cable, building substantial reach requires placing advertising in a variety of media.

Personal video recorders (PVRs) or digital video recorder (DVRs) present another challenge to TV advertising. At present about 11% of the US population owns a PVR/DVR. However, the rate of growth in the past several years is increasing (more than 10% in the past year). Thus, the advertising creative must be sufficiently arresting so that PVR owners do not skip the commercials.

Radio. Radio is a popular medium in the United States. It is estimated that there are 500 million working radios in the U.S. or about 5.5 per household. Ninety-five percent of the cars in the U.S. are equipped with radios. American adults spend more than three hours per day listening to the radio in their homes, cars, and elsewhere. Radio stations cater to the listening tastes of the American public. There are more than 4,400 AM stations, about 3,800 commercial FM stations and approximately 900 public FM stations in the US. In Chicago, for example, the radio listener has a choice of 45 stations. Collectively, these stations offer program formats that include talk, all news, expert-advice, music and discussion. Most consumers are loyal to the one or two stations that offer the preferred program format. Thus, the market share of any station tends to be small and seldom exceeds three percent.

In the last decade, there has been substantial growth in network radio. This growth has been spurred by the availability of syndicated radio shows that offer quality programming. Food, automobile, and drug advertisers are among those who find network radio a viable means of reaching a national audience. The types of radio advertising that can be purchased are the same as those for television: network, spot, and local. Unlike television, the majority of radio advertising is spot and local. Network radio accounts for a small percentage of the radio advertising revenues.

Radio is useful in reaching highly selective audiences. Because there is loyalty to a station, frequency is built readily by repeating an advertising message on the same station. This is advantageous when a product is purchased frequently, because it allows advertising to be aired when consumers are decisional. The frequency provided by radio advertising is also attractive when the goal of advertising is to build an audience's top-of-mind awareness. The ability of radio advertising to deliver frequency combined with its portability makes the medium attractive as a means of reaching consumers with messages in close proximity to when and where they make a brand decision.

Radio enables an advertiser to reach consumers in the morning hours, particularly those consumers who drive to work. For example, between 7 and 8 am, radio attracts over 30% of the population whereas only about 5% of consumers are viewing TV during this time period. In addition, radio also allows quick reaction to changing market conditions. Radio commercials can be produced quickly at a relatively low cost.

Radio has several limitations. It is difficult to build coverage of a target using radio. To do so would require placements on many stations. Radio messages also receive less attention than television commercials. Recall of radio message is about 33% of prime time television commercials and 50% of daytime television commercials. Inattention to radio appeals is due in part to the fact that this medium has substantially more advertising clutter than television (18 minutes of non program material per hour). Inattention is also due to the absence of a visual element, which fosters the tendency for listeners to engage in other activities while attending to the radio.

The growth of radio advertising is threatened by the emergence of satellite radio, which offers 100 channels of digital audio programming throughout the continental United States via satellite that is advertising free. Reception requires a three-band AM/FM/SAT radio, or an adapter for the radio in one's car or home using a portable phone-sized antenna. Listening can also be done on the Internet. Growth has been rapid in the past few years and currently there are 18.5 million subscribers to satellite radio. Because satellite radio provides clear reception throughout the country without advertising, it is likely to compete for a substantial portion of the conventional radio audience.

Interactive Medium: Internet

The Internet has been used as an advertising medium for more than a decade. About 75% of the US population has access to the Internet, though only about 25 have broadband access. Initially, banners were the preferred means of reaching potential customers online. More recently, *paid search* on Google, Yahoo and MSN has accounted for the majority of the online ad expenditures as table 7.2 indicates. Paid search involves payment for the search resulting from a person entering a key word. The more the advertiser is willing to pay at auction, the higher in the list the link to the advertiser appears. *Classifieds* are fees advertisers pay Internet firms to list products or services on vehicles such as online job boards. *Display* advertising involves the payment to an Internet company for a hyper-linked banner or logo on one or more pages. *Lead generation* occurs when advertisers pay Internet advertising companies for qualified purchase inquiries (inquiries by consumers directed at an auto dealer). *Rich media* involves the incorporation of sound, animation or other attention getting devices in advertising. The Internet formats and the percent of ad spending they represent is presented in table 7.2. We focus on paid search in greater detail because it involves major ad expenditures and rich media because of its recent growth.

Format	% of Internet Ad Spending
Paid Search	41%
Classified	17%
Display Ads	21%
Lead Generation	8%
Rich Media	7%

Table 7.2: Ad Spending by Internet Format

Paid Search. In 2009 paid search was at a level of about $14 billion dollars. Currently, paid search occurs predominantly on Google (56%), with smaller representation on Yahoo (19%), MSN (12%), and elsewhere. This reflects the fact that most of the growth in Online advertising has occurred on Google. The cost per click is based on an auction where firms decide how much to bid for placement. The highest bid generally gets the first position on the key words it purchases, though search engines such as Google also give consideration to the relevance of the advertiser for the key words in selecting the order of sites listed on the search engine. To assess the effectiveness of the online search, it is useful to compare against competitive paid searches in terms of the cost for the placement purchased in relation to the hits received (using a service such as hitwise). This analysis allows a comparison of amount paid for position in relation to clicks of all competitors.

To enhance paid search, three strategies should be examined. First is the selection of key words. The choice of broad words will attract substantial clicks, but many of these respondents will not be interested in what they find. This is a problem for the sponsoring firm because the cost of paid search is computed on the number of clicks. A better approach is to select words based on the themes of advertising or the brand's frame of reference. For example, when Audi ran its Godfather ad on the Superbowl, key words including "Godfather," "Godfather Ad," "Audi Commercial" and "R8" were used. Second, the marketing communication that is presented on the landing page should present the brand's position. This helps avoid inappropriate and costly clicks. FTD has several landing pages on the search engine as shown below. The FTD official site is for those who want flowers. Those who want items beyond flowers are likely to click on "Flowers, Roses, Gifts, Gift Baskets," and thus save FTD from making payment for extra clicks (figure 7.1). Finally, consideration should be given to the landing page that is associated with the key word listing on the search engine. If the key word is "Gifts," the search should result in that page popping up on the FTD site rather than the FTD official site home page.

FTD® Official Site
www.FTD.com For Fresh Flowers, Delivered Fast. Rated A+ by Better
Business Bureau.

FTD.**COM - Flowers, Roses, Gifts, Gift Baskets | Fresh Flower Delivery**
Send flowers, roses, gifts, gift baskets and more with convenient
local delivery. Order fresh flowers from *FTD*.com. *www.ftd.com*

Sympathy & Funeral	Flowers
Birthday	Same day delivery
Under $35	Plants
Get Well	Florist Delivered Flowers

Figure 7.1: Search Engine Landing Pages for FTD

A major concern in using paid search is jamming. Jamming
occurs when a competitor or someone else repeatedly clicks on a
brand's link to run up the cost of advertising, lowering that
advertiser's bid to stay within budget, and thus increasing the
opportunity for a competitor to achieve a dominant listing without
having to increase their cost. Search engines attempt to be vigilant to
limit jamming.

Rich Media. The philosophy of how to attract attention to an
ad on a website has evolved in the last decade. Initial efforts involved
the use of interstitials, which are web pages that are displayed before
an expected content page, which typically involved a presentation
that demanded attention before the page of interest could be viewed
(pop-ups) or after it had been seen (pop-unders). Today, less
obtrusive rich media are being used. Advertising presentations
involve animation, sound or other devices to gain attention. For
example a rich media ad for Absolut involved passing a mouse over a
bottle to shake the lemons and reinforce the idea that Absolut has
added a Lemondrop flavor.

Social Networks. Over the past several years a variety of
social networks including Facebook, My Space, and Twitter have
emerged as advertising sites. These social networks enable people to
communicate online with others who subscribe to the network. As
table 7.3 below indicates, Facebook, MySpace and Twitter have a
substantial number of members and good retention of these indivi-

duals. Twitter users tend to be older than those who use Facebook and My Space.

	Facebook	MySpace	Twitter
Worldwide (millions)	200	100	10
US Users (millions)	42	64	4
Retention (monthly%)	67	66	40

Table 7.3: Performance of Major Social Networks, 2009

Advertising on social networks can be done by opening a page featuring the brand or by advertising while users are on the social network. Social networks are attractive because they provide the ability to target more precisely on factors such as age, gender, workplace, relationship status, language. There is an information diffusion element in that when a member signs up as a fan for a brand (often for some incentive) this information is disseminated to all friends of that person. And the social network tracks progress with real-time reporting, thus gaining insight into who is clicking on the brand's ad. The major problem with social networks is that it is a social interaction device where users pay little attention to advertising. Click throughs average less than a third of one percent.

YouTube is a social network that involves the sharing of video materials. Almost 85 million viewers watched 4.3 billion videos on YouTube.com (50.4 videos per viewer) this past year. The average online video duration is just under three minutes. The cost of YouTube advertising depends on the length of time the ad is posted and whether access is direct or through Google AdWords. Although YouTube presents a viable means to develop a viral campaign, the number of people reached is often relatively small and the campaign is open to ads that spoof the brand.

Other Media Alternatives

Out-of Home Advertising. In the past several years, a variety of media have been developed to attract audiences when they were away from home. This includes magazines and TV programming made for doctors' offices. Other locations include health clubs, movie theatres, checkout counters in supermarkets, airplanes (magazines, SkyMall) and on cars that are covered with advertising (autowraps) and driven in designated areas. Surfaces such as truck panels, construction site walls, public restroom walls, airplane seat backs, and tray tables have also been used as advertising space. The success of presenting advertising in these media has been modest. Apparently, consumers are adverse to intrusions when they are doing solitary activities. It may be that the level of current advertising and marketing information, as well as the time famine experienced by most consumers, has made the alternative media more of a nuisance than a desired source of information.

Out-of-home advertising also includes more personal media devices. For example, Lucky Strike, a small and dying brand of cigarettes, rejuvenated interest in its product by introducing the Lucky Strike force. Its members were attractive couples who went around trendy neighborhoods in major cities offering hot coffee, cell phone calls and chairs to smokers who were forced to stand outside while smoking. The result is that Lucky Strike has begun the climb to broader acceptance. In these and many other instances, the goal is to not only to reach target consumers who might not be reached by conventional media, but also to promote favorable word-of-mouth to others who are in the brand's target.

Product Placement. In the past decade, there has been substantial growth in the use of product placement as a means of stimulating brand awareness and liking. The product placement industry exceeds a billion dollars in sales. This involves an advertiser paying to present a brand in the context of a TV program or movie. Various episodes of *Seinfeld* featured J. Peterman, a retailer who offers difficult to find items from around the world. The result was a substantial boost in sales. More recently, the *Desperate Housewives* TV program had the talent wear Halston gowns and had the characters' kitchens equipped with Bosch's Thermador. On the last episode of *Frasier*, he is offered his favorite cookie, Milanos. Whereas early efforts at product placement were at the discretion of program directors, and thus had little to do with the characters or the show's plot, with increased frequency, the script lines are now written by agency personnel. In the case of *Frasier*, a foreign sounding brand fit with Frasier's high brow preferences.

A study by Nielsen indicated that product placement was most effective for audiences who are familiar with the product and who are loyal viewers of the program on which the commercial appears. There is also evidence that when placements are incidental to the story line in the movie or TV program will have limited impact, and highly salient placements can have an adverse effect on consumers' brand attitudes. In cases where the brand does not control the details of the placement, there is the possibility that the placement will associate the brand with some negative event, resulting in unfavorable brand imagery and reduced brand sales. Mercedes Benz envsioned an upscale environment for their brand when they contracted to place one of their cars in the movie *Waiting to Exhale*. What they got was placement in a scene in which a disgruntled woman set fire to her husband's Mercedes Benz.

An important task in designing media strategy is the selection of the media to transmit the advertising message. Media selection is a qualitative decision that is based on numerous factors. These factors are described in more detail in the next chapter. Table 7.4 summarizes the characteristics of the different forms of media described previously.

Summary of Types of Media

This chapter has summarized the different forms of media spanning both traditional and modern modalities. Across media forms, a brand manager can think of the use of static, dynamic, and interactive media forms. However, what tools are at one's disposal for selecting and assessing different media forms? This question will be answered in the next chapter as we delve into media strategy.

		Advantages	Disadvantages
Static	**Magazines**	• Reach target efficiently • High level or reader involvement – ads get more attention • Exceptional catalog value (unlimited exposures) • Good quality color reproductions	• Fairly cluttered • Pass along – readership accumulates slowly • Long lead times to market • More costly than newspaper ads • Readership declining
	Newspapers	• Reaches a large number of people within a geographic area • Self paced; can transmit a lot of info • Exposure is not limited, reader can refer back to ad • Can tailor message to community • Quick turnaround can reflect changing market conditions	• A lot of clutter • Short shelf life • Difficult to target specific groups • Poor reproduction quality • High visibility to competitors • Readership declining
	Outdoor Signage/ Transit	• Broad reach, many will see it repeatedly • Very good for reminding consumers of well known products • Especially effective at enhancing brands when used on conjunction with other mediums	• Difficult to convey substantial info • Hard to measure effectiveness • Difficult/costly to refresh content
	Directories/ Yellow Pages	• Wide availability • Not intrusive • Action oriented, consumers are looking for ads • Relatively inexpensive	• A lot of clutter on pages • Ads often placed near competitors • Ads can not be continually refreshed
Dynamic	**Radio**	• Wide range of programming allows for efficient targeting • Listener loyalty allows advertiser to build frequency • Can reach consumers when they are • decisional • Allows for quick reaction to market conditions • Low cost	• Low market share per station (<3%), may need several stations • Difficult to build coverage of a target • Lower recall than television; more clutter by comparison • Inattention (become background noise)
	Television	• Can reach a lot of people quickly and frequently • Multisensory; opportunity to convey personality of a brand • Can target at the national or regional level	• No catalog value • Substantial number of commercials affects recall • Difficult to achieve broad reach of population • Expensive to create and to update
Interactive	**Internet**	• Broad range with ability for narrow targeting • Rapid growth in user base • Higher conversion rates and ability to track them • Ads do not need to be updated as frequently as with other media • Can be low cost	• Costs contingent on number of clicks in many cases (competitors can influence this) • Increasing amounts of clutter • Obtrusiveness of ads

Table 7.4: Summary of Media Characteristics

Chapter Exercises

- Consider the various media choices described in this chapter. Pick a current brand that you think would benefit from more traditional media exposure and a brand that would benefit from more modern media exposures?

- Consider advertising strategy discussed to this point. What adjustments, if any, need to be made in applying different frameworks to different media forms?

Recommended Reading

Iacobucci, Dawn and Bobby Calder (2003). *Kellogg on Integrated Marketing*. John Wiley & Sons, INc., Hoboken, New Jersey.

Chapter 8

Chapter 8 Objectives

- Strategies for selecting advertising media
- Strategies for selecting advertising vehicles
- Strategies for dominance: matching, monopolizing, mindset, moment
- Developing an advertising budget

This chapter examines the elements of a media strategy from the perspective of a manager who will evaluate a media plan rather than one who assumes responsibility for its development. This is followed by a discussion of the strategic media decisions. First, we examine the criteria for media selection. For example, consider the UPS example discussed at the outset of **Chapter 7**. How does a brand manager or advertiser evaluate the effectiveness of UPS' use of TV, radio, billboards, direct mail and the Internet? This content is followed by a discussion of how the media scheduling decision is made. At issue here is how the specific vehicles within each medium are chosen. In the final section, approaches to developing the advertising budget are enumerated.

Media Selection

Media selection is based on the consideration of the marketing mix a firm is planning to use, the size of the ad budget, competitors' media strategy and consumers' behavior. We begin this analysis by examining the how marketing mix factors shape the choice of media.

The product features that are to be communicated to consumers influence the choice of media. If the product requires demonstration, radio is a poor choice. If promotion of the product requires the delivery of an extensive amount of information about why it should be purchased, static media such as newspapers and magazines are often preferred. The self-paced nature of these media allows consumers to process large amounts of information, whereas dynamic media such as TV and radio do not. Internet presentations that combine static and dynamic elements would also work well, but not static banners.

Distribution is another consideration in media selection. The guideline is that a medium's coverage should match the geographic location of the target. If distribution is regional, network television is typically a poor media choice. Magazines can be employed if distribution is regional, though the cost of reaching each prospect may make this medium unattractive. Radio, spot TV, the Internet and newspapers are usually most viable for regional plans.

Pricing strategy also affects media choice. When there is volatility in pricing, media that allow a firm to react quickly are useful. Media with late closing dates (i.e., allow changes in placement and copy in close proximity to when advertising is aired or printed) afford the needed flexibility. Radio and newspapers have short lead-times. Spot TV allows for some flexibility as do most magazines, though their lead times are greater than for radio and newspapers.

These marketing mix factors are not the only concerns in media selection. The size of the advertising budget often dictates the media that can be used effectively. When budgets are highly limited, television is ruled out as a medium. For example, an ad budget of $1 million could allow as few as three or four insertions per year on network television. This number of insertions is often far too small to establish a strong presence for a brand. When budgets are small, newspaper, radio and Internet advertising are the most attractive of the conventional media. And, even if the advertising budget is substantial, it might impose a limitation on the media used. This can occur when a competitor has sufficient resources to dominate a medium with advertising. Thus, a small fast food brand such as Quiznos should consider the fact that its competition is McDonald's and Burger King, both of whom engage in substantial advertising. Less used media might be appropriate to compete against these brands.

Legal restraints also play a role in media selection. Some products cannot be advertised on television. Among these are cigarettes and, until recently, all hard liquor. For other products, the various media make determinations about the suitability of advertising for public consumption. A GoDaddy spot was not permitted in the Superbowl because it was thought to be in bad taste for family viewing.

A final consideration in media selection is consumers' behavior. If consumers make buying decisions over an extensive period of time (e.g., furniture), print media that allow consumers to catalog the advertising is preferred to broadcast which is fleeting. If consumers make a purchase at a point in time and without much deliberation, as is the case for automobile tires and barbecue sauce, an intrusive medium that delivers an audience instantaneously is desirable. Broadcast media are thus often preferred in this case.

The factors considered in choosing media are presented in figure 8.1. As the above analysis suggests, media selection typically involves ruling out media that do not meet one or more of the criteria, and then assessing the virtues of those media that remain.

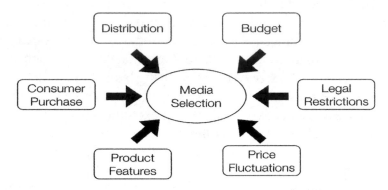

Figure 8.1: Criteria for Selection of Media

Vehicle Selection

Once a decision has been made with regard to advertising media, vehicles are selected. Vehicles are an intra-medium concept and describe the choice within a specific medium. For TV, a vehicle might be a commercial placement in prime time or late night, for radio, it might be drive time, for magazines it might be Time, and for the Internet it might be Google search. Vehicles that are highly efficient in exposing the target to advertising are generally preferred. To identify such vehicles, it is necessary to know the size and composition of the audiences they attract.

In selecting vehicles, the strategist's hope is that appropriate choices will ensure brand preference or at least brand awareness. But these outcomes are not for sale! None of the above measures pertains to advertising exposure. In purchasing space, the number of people exposed to the medium in which advertising is placed is the measure used. The assumption is that if consumers are exposed to a vehicle, they will also be exposed to the advertising within that vehicle and perhaps be influenced by it. This assumption is necessary because measuring advertising exposures and effects directly would be prohibitively expensive. For strategic purposes, vehicle exposure is then qualified by comparing vehicles in terms of the cost per 1000 people reached who are in the target.

Below, we examine procedures for estimating the size and composition of vehicle audiences. Print estimation procedures are discussed first. This is followed by a description of the estimation procedures used for broadcast vehicles.

Audience Estimation for Print

One way to estimate the readership for print vehicles is to use circulation data. Various services such as the Audit Bureau of Circulation (ABC) and Standard Rates and Data Services (SRDS) routinely publish circulation data for consumer magazines. For example, ABC reports the number of copies of a vehicle that were printed, the paid circulation in subscription and newsstands, promotional copies, renewals and new subscriptions. This information permits an assessment of the quality of circulated copies on the assumption that the greater the paid circulation, the more attractive the vehicle. SRDS also reports circulation data for farm books, and Business Publications Audit of Circulation provides circulation information for business publications. Circulation simply indicates how many units have been received by readers.

For assessing advertising, an audience measure is typically used. Audience refers to the number of people exposed to a vehicle. Thus, an audience includes people who subscribe to a vehi-cle as well as pass-along. Audiences are estimated through surveys where a representative sample of consumers must exhibit their familiarity with the print vehicle under consideration to be counted as a member of the audience. *Effective* audience refers to the number of people exposed to a magazine who have the target demographic and geographic characteristics. Effective audience is the critical measure in assessing various vehicle alternatives. The attempt is to find vehicles that disproportionately reach people with the same profile as those in the target per thousand people reached by the vehicle.

Audience Estimation for Television

Syndicated services provide audience estimates for tele-vision programs. The most popular of these services is provided by the Nielsen Company. Nielsen recruits a sample of about 25,000 representative homes from around the country for national ratings. An electronic device called a people-meter is placed in each home attached to the occupant's TV set. It is used to keep track of whether the TV set is on or off and the channel to which it is tuned. Also, viewers input a code to indicate who is watching (kids do not do so reliably). In addition, Nielsen collects 1.6 million hand-written diaries of people's viewing habits. Arbitron also offers a competitive service that uses a diary to estimate ratings and has a meter system to measure viewing.

To illustrate the types of data available from the Nielsen service, consider a situation in which there are 10 homes. These homes can tune in one of three channels. As table 8.1 indicates, three homes are tuned to Program 1, two to Program 2, and two to Program 3. One home does not have a working set, and two homes have the TV turned off. Several measures are collected:

Household		Program		
		Program 1	Program 2	Program 3
1. No Working Set		0	0	0
2. Not Turned On		0	0	0
3. Turned on to Program 1		1	0	0
4. Turned on to Program 2		0	1	0
5. Turned on to Program 3		0	0	1
6. Turned on to Program 1		1	0	0
7. Turned on to Program 2		0	1	0
8. Turned on to Program 3		0	0	1
9. Turned on to Program 1		1	0	0
10. Not Turned On		0	0	0

Table 8.1: Measures of TV Program Viewership

- *Houses Using Television or HUT.* In table 8.1, HUT is 70%. HUT increases gradually during the day and peaks during prime time at about 60% of households before declining. Another measure is

People Using Television (PUT), which is based on the individual using television rather than the household.

- *Share of audience.* This measure is often used to determine whether a program stays on the air. The particular number that determines the fate of a show varies by network and time slot. It is computed by dividing the percent of homes turned to a program by HUT. Thus, the share of audience for Program 1 in table 8.1 is 30%/70% or 43%. Network programs with shares under 10 are usually short-lived.

- *Rating.* This refers to the percent of all homes tuned to a particular program. Here the assumption is that all households have TVs. The rating for Program 1 in table 8.1 is 30%. Advertisers are most interested in the rating measure in selecting television vehicles.

Several observations about the above measures of viewership are worthy of further discussion. From a conceptual standpoint, HUT and PUT are measures of circulation and rating is a measure of audience size. Most advertisers are not interested in the ratings per se. As noted above, ratings provide the advertiser with a measure of the audience. Of greater interest is the rating for a particular target or segmentation of the population. For this purpose, Nielsen provides demographic data similar to that available for print. And it offers continual data in 55 major markets.

Table 8.2 summarizes the elements of vehicle selection for print as well as television advertisements that a manager should consider evaluating when analyzing the potential media plan. These elements include circulation, audience, and effective audien-ce.

Media Scheduling

To this point, we have viewed vehicle selection as if it were done in isolation. The vehicle that most efficiently delivers the target audience would presumably be selected. Indeed, this would be the case if a schedule were composed of a single vehicle. Most schedules, however, involve multiple insertions in a particular vehicle and inser-

tions in several vehicles. Thus, vehicle selection requires a consideration of the complementarity of vehicles in fulfilling some objective.
We now turn to scheduling across multiple vehicles.

	Circulation	Audience	Effective Audience
Definition	The number of physical units through which the advertising is distributed	The number of people who are exposed to the vehicle used to transmit advertising	The number of people with the target's characteristics who are exposed to the vehicle used to transmit advertising
For Print	Readership data from the ABC or SRDS	Subscribers + Pass Along; often ad familiarity surveys are used to assess this	Measured by a consumer survey of demographics and psychographics
For Television	HUT and PUT measures	Ratings; usually obtained through a syndicated service such as Nielson	Measured by consumer survey of demographics and psychographics

Table 8.2: Considerations for Vehicle Selection

Reach, Average Frequency, and Tonnage

To develop a media schedule, several concepts are needed.
These include reach and average frequency. These concepts refer to
exposures during *any particular month.*

o *Reach* refers to the total number of unique people or households
that will be exposed to a schedule at least once over a specified
period of time. Reach is primarily discussed in terms of a four-
week period.

o *Average frequency* refers to the average number of times a person
or household is exposed to a schedule. A mean and an estimate of
variance about the mean specify average frequency.

Consider the placement of two print ads, one in *Time* and one in *Newsweek*. First, SMRB or some other service (typically subscribed to by large advertisers and agencies) is consulted to determine the size of the audience for each magazine. The audience (circulation + pass along) is 20 million people for *Time* and 15 million for *Newsweek*. Using only this information, the tonnage or total number of exposures can be computed. For print this tonnage is called Gross Audience.

$$\text{Gross Audience} = \sum (\text{insertions x audience})$$
$$= (20 \text{ X } 1 + 15 \text{ X } 1)$$
$$= 35 \text{ Million}$$

It should be noted, however, that the reach need not be 35 million. In fact, reach would be 35 million only if there were no overlap in readership between *Time* and *Newsweek*. Usually there is overlap across vehicles, which is called duplication. To estimate reach, duplication must be subtracted from Gross Audience. To determine duplication, the syndicated service data are consulted. SMRB reports pairwise duplication (e.g. *Time*, *Newsweek*) in their data books. For more complicated situations, say the duplication for four books, individual respondents' data are examined electronically. Suppose it is found that duplication is 5 million as shown in figure 8.2. Thus, the two vehicle schedule provides 35 million exposures, reaches 30 million people, and reaches each person with an average frequency of 1.17 times.

Several questions are prompted by this analysis. What should the level of average frequency be? It depends on a number of factors, and most importantly, how often are consumers decisional about the category? The more frequently they make decisions, the greater the frequency that is needed. We shall examine these criteria in detail later in this chapter. Another issue is whether a gross audience is a useful basis for deciding on a vehicle. Typically strategists are interested in effective audience, that is, consumers with the target profile who are exposed to a vehicle. The analysis of effective audience is the same as it is for gross audience.

Gross Audience

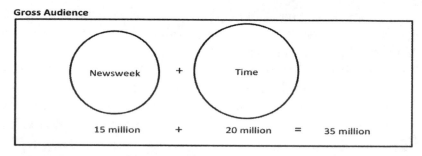

Reach (Unique Readers)

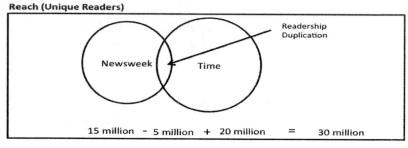

Average Frequency

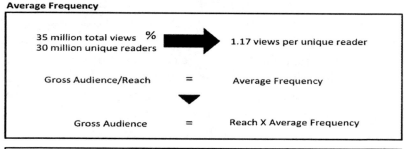

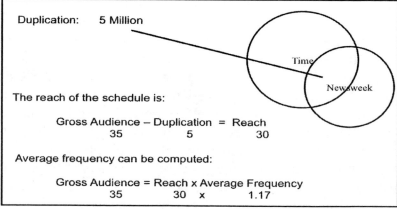

Figure 8.2: Computing Average Frequency

A similar analysis is employed in designing broadcast schedules. To illustrate the approach, consider placements on two half hour television programs with ratings of 60 and 40 (meaning 60% and 40% of all homes are watching these program when they air). For broadcast media, the tonnage is called Gross Rating Points (GRPs). Here tonnage as expressed by GRPs measures the sum of the ratings for a particular placement. A GRPs of 100 can be thought of as reaching the entire audience on average one time.

$$\text{GRPs} = \Sigma(\text{insertions x ratings})$$
$$100 = (60 \times 1 + 40 \times 1)$$

However, this is only a conceptual definition. In actuality, GRPs of 100 can be varied so that most of the audience is reached a few times or a small percent of the audience reached many times as the following equation implies.

$$\text{GRPs} = \text{Reach x Average Frequency}$$
$$100 = 60 \times 1.67$$

Here, the 100 GRP schedule reaches 60% of the households on average 1.67 times.

Several aspects of the foregoing analysis warrant discussion. First, it should be recognized that the computation of reach and average frequency would be the same as that illustrated if the schedule were composed of repeated insertions in the same vehicle. Second, an important consideration in selecting among potential schedules is to select the one that delivers the desired reach and average frequency with minimum variance about the average frequency. If two schedules offer identical GRPs, reach and average frequency, the vehicles offering the least dispersion about the average frequency are selected. When the goal is to reach people an average of three times, then it is preferable to reach all people three times. This is usually not possible. But the less the deviation is from the target, the greater the impact of a schedule.

Reach vs. Frequency

Our analysis of reach and frequency indicates that for any particular level of GRP level, reach must be decreased to enhance frequency. Advertisers have long debated this tradeoff. In the 1970s, it was common to favor a reach approach. Budgets tended to be sufficient to ensure reasonable frequency and still get high levels of reach. The preferred number during the 1970s and '80s was at least three exposures, which is referred to as the "three plus frequency rule." This rule was presumably based on a 1979 Association of National Advertisers' (ANA) study. But the investigator responsible for that study, Michael Naples states: "What I said was that each brand should...figure out what its own curve was."

A General Electric researcher, Herb Krugman, also advocated three exposures, but what he was referring to was three types of exposures. The first type gets people to say "what is it?" We have discussed this question in terms of frame of reference. The second type of exposure gets people to say "what of it?" This question was discussed in terms of points of difference. And the third exposure prompts a decision. Thus, Krugman's argument was not that three was the right number of ad exposures, but that consumers responded to mounting exposures in three different ways. The number of exposures that make people decisional is an empirical question and varies by both brand and category.

In the late 1990s, a new rule of thumb emerged. Based on research with selected brands, the conclusion emerged that a single exposure to an ad is the appropriate level of frequency. This is generally referred to as the C-curve because of the shape of the response function (figure 8.3). The C-curve implies that frequency should always be traded for reach as the value of an additional exposure is lower than the value of reaching another person.

Evidence for the C-curve has been found in several studies. These have been for major brands in their category that have had a stable position and a long-lived advertising campaign. Reach makes sense in this situation. However, it is inappropriate to conclude that all brands follow the C-curve. There is a wealth of data to deny this conclusion.

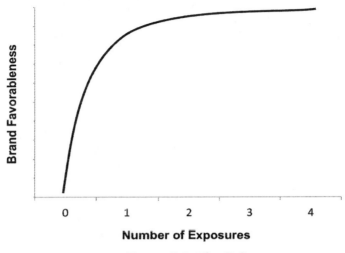

Figure 8.3: The C-Curve

There is considerable evidence to indicate that in most cases some repetition of advertising enhances consumers' responses. This outcome is not surprising from an information processing perspective. Repetition enhances both amplification and recency, the two factors thought to stimulate the accessibility of information in long-term memory. Very substantial levels of repetition have been shown to foster wearout, that is, people become less favorable toward a product as repetitions mount. We refer to this response function as the S-curve (figure 8.4; see portion of curve between 0 and 5 exposures, which resembles an S).

Advertising Wearout. Wearout is thought to occur because once people have learned the information an ad has to convey, they use additional ad exposures as an opportunity to scrutinize the message assertions by comparing it to other things they know. Or, they may simply dismiss the information as old news and not think about it. In either event, what is rehearsed is likely to be less favorable than the information presented in the ad. This results in wearout.

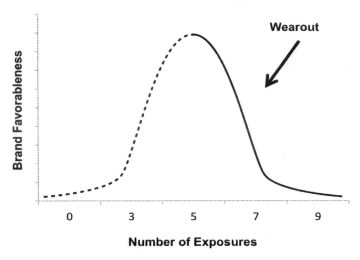

Figure 8.4: S-Curve and Wearout Phenomenon

Figure 8.4 illustrates a situation where beyond five exposures wearout sets in. Wearout is particularly common in radio advertising, because this medium tends to attract a loyal audience that is exposed to the same ads repeatedly. It is also common in business-to-business advertising, where the low unit cost of space prompts advertisers to place a substantial number of insertions in each issue.

The most common approach used by advertisers who are susceptible to wearout is to change the context in which advertising is presented while sustaining the same theme. For example, a soft drink producer might emphasize thirst quenching in all of the commercials included in a campaign, but use different scenes and actors to deliver this appeal. This approach is often ineffective in the short term. What appears to happen is that people process the message information in response to the first few exposures. Thereafter, they activate their own repertoire of product-related associations. Because messages are designed to be highly persuasive, the processing of message inform-ation is likely to lead to a more favorable disposition toward the product than the activation of individuals' own repertoire of asso-ciations. Thus wearout occurs. This is not to say that a change in setting is never effective in forestalling wearout, but rather this device is likely to be effective only if the different contexts offer consumers news.

Rules of Thumb. Our analysis indicates that a simple rule of thumb about the appropriate level of frequency is unlikely to result in an effective media strategy. There are many considerations that underlie the choice of the reach and frequency level. Some of these are summarized in table 8.3. Most of these criteria are self-explanatory. However, the meaning of planned vs. unplanned requires some elaboration. An unplanned purchase implies that people have no intention of using the brand now or in the future. Unforeseen events prompt them to consider it. For most consumers, purchase of cough medicine is unplanned. They do not foresee getting a cough, have no intention of buying a cough medicine, and thus are not interested in advertising by cough syrups. At the onset of a cough, they become more attentive to information about cough medicines. To attract these consumers, frequency is needed so that the advertising is present when the unforeseen event occurs.

	Circumstance	Frequency	Reach
Consumer	Purchase Cycle	Short	Long
	Purchase Decision	Unplanned	Planned
	Interest	Low	High
	Loyalty	Low	High
Competition	Point of Purchase	Many Brands	Few Brands
	Price	Relatively High	Relatively Low
	Quality	Parity	Superior
Creative	Complexity	Complex	Simple
	Campaign Maturity	New	Old
Media	Environment	Cluttered	Uncluttered

Table 8.3: Circumstances When Reach and Frequency are Appropriate

This is not to say that a particular category is planned or unplanned. Cough syrups might be a planned purchase for households in which there are children. If this were the case, a reach strategy would be appropriate. The framework in table 8.3 helps to determine when a reach or a frequency strategy is most useful. For example, if the purchase cycle is short, such as with barbeque sauce, a frequency strategy works best as the consumer receives numerous exposures during the time when they are decisional, whereas if the purchase cycle is long such as is typically the case for the purchase of a car, a reach strategy would be most appropriate.

Concentration vs. Continuity

Media scheduling involves not only decisions about where to advertise, but also about when to advertise. Reach and frequency are used to decide where advertising is placed in a particular month. Continuity vs. concentration address when to spend the ad budget over the year. Thus, the ad budget is allocated to reach, frequency and continuity. Spending on one of these strategies involves reducing the spending on one or both of the others.

Continuity involves spending the ad budget relatively evenly throughout the year. The alternative is a concentration strategy that could be used where advertising dollars are spent during a single period. Historically, advertisers used a concentration strategy for seasonal products and continuity otherwise. However, as the cost of media began to rise at a faster rate than advertising budgets, two other approaches became common: flighting and pulsing. *Flighting* involves advertising for some period, followed by a hiatus with no advertising and then by a second flight. *Pulsing* entails the same general approach as flighting, except that low levels of advertising replace the hiatuses. The idea in flighting and pulsing is to deliver the impact of concentration with the sustaining value of continuity. Figure 8.4 depicts continuity over the year and flighting approaches.

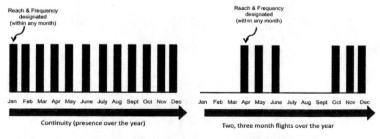

Figure 8.4: Continuity and Flighting

Concentration has the virtue of delivering a substantial presence. However, there is likely to be significant forgetting during the periods when there is no advertising. This state of affairs would seem acceptable only when dealing with a seasonal product, and even then caution is warranted in using concentration. Too often advertisers use concentration in the belief that sales are seasonal, in effect exacerbating seasonality.

To illustrate this point, consider the experience of a soft drink manufacturer about 25 years ago. Category sales were seasonal, with 65 percent of sales occurring during the period May to October. Soft drink advertisers spent the vast majority of their ad budgets against this season. In an attempt to alter this pattern, one soft drink producer experimented with a more balanced budget by advertising contraseasonally. The result was increased non-seasonal consumption and sustained seasonal consumption. Apparently there was not a compelling reason for soft drink seasonality. Disproportionate advertising against the summer season became a self-fulfilling prophecy that ensured continued seasonality. Other soft drink manufacturers quickly changed to a more balanced spending pattern. As a result, the six-month soft drink season accounts for less than 60% of annual sales today.

Whether concentration or continuity is being considered, an important issue in planning a media schedule is how to space repeated exposures to advertising. There is emerging evidence that as you increase the time interval between exposures to an ad, you increase the perception that the information contained in the ad is unfamiliar, and this enhances the likelihood that the audience will pay attention to the advertising. The implication is that the spacing of repeated exposures operates in the same way as exposures themselves, that is, by affecting the resources available for message processing. Like increases in repetition, increases in the inter-exposure interval enhance the resources available for information processing. However, there comes a point where the interval between exposures is so large that there is little savings of the information learned from prior advertising exposures. In this event, each exposure acts like an initial exposure. In addition, there are times when it is important to concentrate advertising. Such loading within a month occurs when introducing a new product (e.g., new model cars), or at the end of a season when it is important to reduce inventory (e.g., hot cereal in March).

Strategies for Dominance

In developing a media plan, it is important to make media choices that enhance the likelihood that advertising will be noticed and used as a basis for choice. For large advertisers, such dominance can often be achieved by out-shouting the competitor, that is, by buying more reach, frequency and continuity. For all advertisers, four factors should be examined in developing a media plan that allows competitive dominance: Matching, monopolizing, mindset and moment (see figure 8.5).

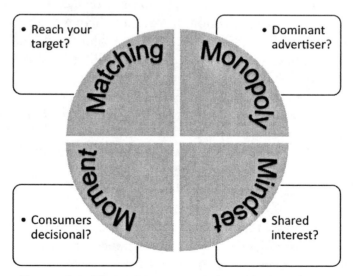

Figure 8.5: The 4M Framework for Vehicle Selection

Traditionally, advertisers chose media that provided efficient coverage of the target; that is, they emphasized a matching goal. This entails identifying the target's demographics and selecting vehicles that are most efficient in matching these demographics. Efficiency is measured in the cost per thousand target individuals (CPMs). The lower the CPMs, the more attractive the vehicle. Monopoly involves choosing media so that when the brand is advertising, competitive products (and ideally all brands) are not advertising. Because competitors often target the same people, the same media are most efficient for all competitors. Brands with smaller budgets thus must seek alternative and usually somewhat less efficient vehicles to achieve a monopoly. Narrowing the target often reduces the variety of vehicles needed and thus allows monopolizing of the consumers who are targeted. Narrowing the geographical scope of advertising is another targeting device that can be used to monopolize competition. Monopolizing might also be achieved through the media strategies developed. This might entail focusing advertising during one period of time. Although Sunkist soft drink is purchased year round by consumers, the brand advertises heavily at the beginning of the season (April/May) to ensure that the brand advertising is dominant in the soft drink category despite Sunkist's relatively small ad budget.

More recently, two additional criteria for choosing media have emerged. One is mindset. Here the idea is to select media that reflect a shared interest. This can be achieved in a number of different ways. One is *affiliation*. For example, Marlboro sponsored a NASCAR race car, highlighting the notion that Marlboro and its consumers had a shared interest in racing. UPS' use of Dale Jarrett as a spokesperson resonates with UPS customers who value NASCAR, and the UPSalamode website underscores UPS's commitment to the fashion industry. Mindset can also be achieved by creating *intimacy* with the target. Along these lines, Marlboro has a contest where entrants provide information about themselves in order be included in a drawing for a vacation on a dude ranch. This prize is a means of affiliation. In addition, Marlboro sends contestants birthday cards with coupons that can be redeemed for Marlboro coupons, thus building intimacy. Finally, in some cases mindset is achieved by having consumers serve as advocates for the brand. TREMOR is a Procter and Gamble creation that has attracted several hundred thousand teens (http://tremor.com/index.html). TREMOR members are given products and coupons with the hope that they will advocate them to other people. For example, TREMOR teen girls might be given a coupon for a beauty product in the hope that they and their friends (who do not have coupons) will go to a retail outlet to try the product. Similarly, there are adult advocacy sites such as bzzagent and Vocal Point that provide vehicles for adult advocacy of brands they favor.

Moment involves reaching people when they are likely to be decisional about the category. For example, Tide might advertise in laundromats to reach people when they are thinking about and perhaps selecting a detergent, and L'Oreal might advertise its makeup on subways to reach women when they are returning home and perhaps planning their evening activities. To identify when people are decisional it is often helpful to conduct ethnographic studies, which track people over a period of time to identify when they are thinking about the category in which a brand holds membership.

Budgeting

How much should a firm spend on advertising? An accurate estimate of how much to spend on advertising requires empirical research. But even if such an investigation is contemplated, some budget levels must be selected for test purposes. There are rules of thumb that provide rough estimates of how much to spend on advertising. We review these rules next but ultimately one's budgeting also depends on one's experience and empirical data.

Budgeting Rules of Thumb

Perhaps the most common rule of thumb to estimate the ad budget is percent of sales. A recent survey indicated about 50% of the largest advertisers in the U.S. use this approach to budget estimation. It involves estimating the sales for the next year and multiplying that number by some percent of sales that has been used traditionally by the firm. For Coca-Cola, this figure might be 3%, whereas for a Kellogg's cereal it might be as high as 10%. The percent of sales is useful in that it provides a ballpark estimate of what might be spent on advertising. It is easy to compute and easy to justify to management when the percentage chosen can be related to historical spending. But it is based on the premise that sales cause advertising rather than the reverse, and it might not reflect the objectives set for advertising. For example, a budget based on percent of sales might lead a firm to reduce advertising in anticipation or response to declining sales, which might be the very situation when an increase in the ad expenditure is needed.

Another rule of thumb is competitive emulation. Following this approach, a firm tracks competitors' ad spending and emulates competitors in terms of the absolute advertising expenditure or some percent of competitive expenditure. The tracking of competitors' expenditures is facilitated by services such as Leading National Advertisers (LNA) and Broadcast Advertising Reports (BAR reports). These services provide data related to ad expenditures by brand. Competitive emulation is a useful approach in that it focuses a firm on its share of advertising voice (SOV), that is, its ad expenditure vs. the expenditure by all advertisers in the category. Low SOV levels have been found to stimulate demand for the category rather than for the firm's brand. For a number of years, B.F. Goodrich's low SOV and the similarity in its name to the leading tire manufacturer, Goodyear, resulted in Goodrich ad expenditures enhancing Goodyear sales! Competitive emulation might reduce the chances of this happening. However, competitive emulation per se is a poor approach to budgeting because it assumes competitors know the appropriate amount to spend and that a firm is in the same market circumstance as the company it is emulating. Further, in the absence of special market intelligence, emulation is delayed until competitors' expenditures can be determined, at which time emulation might no longer be appropriate.

Another rule of thumb is all you can afford. This involves calculating all the marketing costs and then allocating what remains to advertising. All you can afford is typically invoked when a firm has limited resources to spend on marketing and uses the rule of thumb to determine the ad expenditure. Although resource availability is a limiting factor in the ad budget allocation, focusing on advertising as the first place to cut expenditures may be short sighted. Conversely, spending what you can afford might be more than is appropriate in relation to the opportunity available.

Empirical Approaches to Budgeting

Fortunately, a variety of research procedures are available to help in determining the appropriate ad budget. Typically, when these procedures are followed, budget assessment is but one of the concerns being addressed empirically. The choice among procedures involves tradeoffs in the cost, time to conduct the research, and accuracy of the results.

Perhaps the most thorough and costly approach to budget estimation involves the use of test markets. Two criteria are considered. One is the representativeness of the city. In some cases, cities are chosen because they are representative of the country as a whole, and in other cases because they represent some segment of interest such as high brand or category development. The other criterion for test market selection is containment. This refers to the extent to which the effect of some marketing effort can be localized. At issue is the extent to which advertising and distribution will be limited to the test city. Dayton, Ohio offers good containment because advertising in this city covers only the city and because product placed in Dayton is likely to be sold only in Dayton and not shipped to other cities. Once the cities are selected, the effect of different budgets can be compared by randomly assigning different cities to different budget levels.

An alternative to the conventional test market is the controlled cable test market. Services such as Behaviorscan by IRI have set up test cities in which they have split TV cable going to consumers' homes. This allows Behaviorscan clients to vary the message, advertising weight, and media schedule going to different homes. Behaviorscan also collects scanner data at supermarkets and links this information to the consumers who make the purchase. In this way, it is possible to relate the extent to which different levels of advertising budget affect individual consumption. Behaviorscan is thus a powerful device that is underutilized by consumer packaged goods companies. Unfortunately, although empirically sound, firms are deterred by its high cost (about $300,000).

Despite the virtues of split cable systems, they are not always attractive. When consumption occurs in outlets other than supermarkets, other testing procedures are needed. The split cable test cities are few in number and thus might not be representative of the locales to which you wish to project. For example, the test cities might be ones where your brand is already strong. In this event, the chances of detecting an effect of advertising are reduced. This outcome might cause a firm to scrap a marketing program when in fact it might have been a successful program in all but the saturated markets.

Although test markets are effective for planning an advertising budget, they are expensive. A less expensive alternative to budget estimation involves using correlational analysis. This involves examining the co-variation in a firm's ad expenditures and sales. In a growing number of firms, the databases are now available to do such analyses on a market-by-market basis. This allows the advertiser to focus the expenditure on those markets where there is high co-variation between ad expenditure and sales during times of tight ad budgets. The problem with using co-variation to infer the appropriate ad budget is that there is no assurance that it is the advertising that caused the response.

Summary of Media Strategy

Media strategy involves three steps. Initially media are selected. We suggested that this is achieved by examining elements of the marketing mix (product, price, distribution), the ad budget, legal constraints, and the target's behavior. Media that do not accommodate these factors are eliminated, and a selection is made from the remaining media. Thus, the selection of media is qualitative. In contrast, vehicle selection is primarily quantitative. It entails selecting vehicles that match the profile of the target and minimize the cost per thousand of reaching the target. Finally, media scheduling involves the selection of vehicles that achieve the desired reach and frequency during each month of the year, and provide the continuity or concentration needed over the year. In developing the media strategy, consideration is given to assure the relevance of the advertising. This is achieved by considering matching, monopolizing, mindset and moment. Budgeting often involves using rules of thumb to determine the general level of spending. These rules reflect a consideration of the anticipated sales, competitive spending and the advertising resources available to a brand.

Chapter Exercises

- You have started a business that involves importing woven scarves and ties from India. Your ad budget of $250,000. What media would you select to advertise these products?

- What media would you consider to advertise *Head & Shoulders* dandruff shampoo to teen and young adult men? Focus on moment and mindset as the basis for your selection.

- All of the advertising is concentrated in June for a new sunscreen. Is this a reach or frequency strategy? Do you agree with the continuity of the strategy?

- A Chicago-based executive master's program has decided to advertise its weekend certificate program. The target is adults in their 30s who do not have an MBA degree and who live within 200 miles of Chicago. The program is situated in Chicago, Illinois and advertises in newspapers. The advertising is placed in the *Chicago Tribune* and *Chicago Sun Times*, the *Milwaukee Journal Sentinel*, and the *Wisconsin State Journal* (Madison). In each outlet, there are four insertions of half page advertising per week during March, April, May, August and September. The cost of these insertions is $50,000. The dean has cut the budget in half. What recommendations would you make to accommodate the new budget?

Recommended Readings

Anand, Punam and Brian Sternthal (1990), "Ease of Message Processing as a Moderator of Repetition Effects in Advertising," *Journal of Marketing Research*, 17, 345-353.

Malaviya, Prashant (2007), "The Moderating Influence of Advertising Context on Ad Repetition Effects: The Role of Amount and Type of Elaboration," *Journal of Consumer Research*, 34, 32-40.

Malaviya, Prashant and Brian Sternthal (1997), "The Persuasive Impact of Message Spacing," *Journal of Consumer Psychology*, 6, 233-255.

Schumann, David, Richard E. Petty, and D. Scott Clemons (1990), "Predicting the Effectiveness of Different Strategies of Advertising Variation: A Test of the Repetition-variation Hypotheses," *Journal of Consumer Research*, 17, 192-202.

Creative Strategy

Chapter 9

Chapter 9 Objectives

- Evaluate message structure strategies for message amplification: Hard/soft sell, big idea, story grammar, comparative advertising, and analogies
- Evaluate spokespeople based strategies for message amplification: Attractive, expert and trustworthy spokespeople
- Assess strategies for motivating amplification: Threat and humor

Green Giant positioned its frozen vegetables as being fresher than those of the competition. At issue was how to communicate their positioning of freshness in the TV advertising they were planning. Should the ad execution focus on freshness and reiterate this point throughout the commercial? What would get consumers to pay attention to a low involvement product category such as frozen vegetables? Should a spokesperson testify to the freshness of the vegetables? Should humor be used? Some device was needed if information about Green Giant was to break through the boredom barrier and get target consumers to amplify on the freshness benefit.

Green Giant and its ad agency, Leo Burnett, ruled out using an actor to inform consumers about Green Giant's freshness. It was reasoned that consumers did not take frozen vegetables seriously and neither should the advertising for the brand. The fear was that having a person inform the consumer about vegetables would be viewed as pedantic by consumers. Instead an animated character, Sprout, was introduced to represent the consumer. Sprout was uninformed about what made vegetables fresh so he was eager to learn this information. In each commercial, Sprout learned of another reason why the brand was fresh. This was expected to be more palatable to consumers than having a person reciting the reasons to believe Green Giant was fresh. And to help consumers remember that the commercial was for Green Giant, Sprout appeared in all the ads, the Green Giant was shown in the background, and the brand's quality was always discussed.

In this chapter, we examine creative strategies to enhance the chances that consumers learn the brand's position and are persuaded by it. This entails developing strategies for amplification, that is, strong associations to the brand's benefit. And because amplification requires significant effort, we examine strategies that stimulate consumers' attention to the advertising.

The Importance of Message Amplification

Message amplification reflects both the type and amount of message-related thought in which consumers engage. The type of thought involved in amplification can be positive, neutral, or negative toward a message advocacy. For example, an advertisement for Clearasil acne medication might show a before and after picture to demonstrate the effectiveness of the product. Some consumers might amplify this information by thinking positive thoughts, "The product helps reduce acne," whereas others who saw the same commercial might think, "The product didn't completely eliminate the person's acne." Still others might generate thoughts unrelated to the message, "The person in the ad seems familiar. Have I seen this person before?" Such positive, neutral and negative thoughts form the basis of consumers' attitudes. Consumers' attitudes become more positive as the proportion of positive to negative and neutral thoughts increases. And a more positive a consumer's attitude toward a brand, the greater is the likelihood of its purchase.

Amplification also pertains to the amount of thinking. The greater the amount of thinking that is done in response to a message, the greater the cognitive resources that are needed. At the same time, the allocation of significant resources does not necessarily result in greater processing of the message content because the consumer could be focusing on the music or colors presented in the ad rather than allocating resources to the information or implications of the message itself. As noted in our discussion of wearout in the last chapter, the resources might also be used to think about things other than what is said in the message such as a prior experience with the product. In addition, the amount of message-related amplification that occurs depends on what consumers know about the category and the brand: The greater their knowledge, the greater the amplification possible. And this amplification need not occur only at the time of the execution. Consumers might also think about advertisements later or discuss them with friends, which could promote additional amplification.

The key tasks in developing creative strategy is to design a message that (a) evokes positive message-related thoughts from the target audience, (b) fosters the amplification of these thoughts, and (c) limits the amplification of thoughts antagonistic to the message. The starting assumption in developing this discussion is that the brand positioning has been developed in a compelling manner, which makes the focus on creative execution appropriate.

Using Message Structure to Prompt Message Amplification

There are various approaches to structuring the presentation of the message content to foster its amplification by consumers. We examine some of the more frequently used devices. In doing so, we also discuss when each approach is likely to be effective as well as precautions that should be considered in adopting the strategy.

Hard Sell (Soft Sell)

Hard sell is a technique that was developed in the 1960s and credited to Rosser Reeves of the Ted Bates Advertising Agency. It involves advertising in which a simple associative bond is developed between a brand and its functional benefit: "buy this brand, get this benefit." Advertising for Rolaids, for example, uses a hard sell by introducing the slogan "Rolaids spells relief." Similarly, M&Ms candy used a hard sell by promising that "It melts in your mouth not on your hands." By announcing the brand and its benefit, a hard sell strengthens the associative bond between the brand name and the brand benefit. It is an effective approach to amplification when a brand possesses a point of difference that is important to consumers. In contrast, in the absence of a point of difference, hard sell is not effective. When Bates was hired to advertise for an airline that did not have a point of difference important to consumers, the agency struggled to develop effective advertising, and they eventually lost the account.

A variant of the hard sell approach is called the soft sell (see work by Rucker and Galinsky, 2009). Whereas the hard sell emphasizes the functional benefit provided by an advertisement, the soft sell instead proposes that the product is appealing because it conveys a particular status or image. However, the logic of the approach is the same as that for hard sell, but associates an image rather than an attribute with the brand. For example, Mercedes, in one print campaign, emphasizes the image and status of those who own the car rather than the functional features of the vehicle.

A limitation of both the hard and soft sell approaches lies in their simplicity. That is, because the message is easy to apprehend, consumers are not likely to have much information to elaborate on in subsequent exposures. Thus, after consumers have learned the attribute or image, there is risk that they will disengage from the advertising perhaps by generating thoughts unrelated to the message.

The Big Idea: Convergent Attributes or Benefits

The "Big Idea" approach to amplification was pioneered by the Leo Burnett ad agency. It involves identifying a functional benefit that is important to consumers (often the benefit is one that defines a category), and over time presenting a variety of attributes that are reasons to believe the benefit. At the same time, the context is kept constant so that people can readily associate the ad with the brand name, ensuring strong brand linkage. We term this approach Big Idea I.

Advertising for Green Giant described at the outset of this chapter illustrates the application of the Big Idea I. The setting is always in the valley and features a cartoon animation, so that consumers know at the outset of the ad that Green Giant is the sponsor. The reliable use of this context, and the fact that the benefit is always superior freshness, link the individual executions together as a campaign. By changing the attributes that support this benefit over time, news is provided to sustain consumer interest (figure 9.1). Along these lines, successive generations of ads feature the fact that Green Giant vegetables are fresh frozen, vacuum-packed, and packed in butter sauce to imply superior freshness.

The Big Idea prompts amplification by relating a variety of attributes to the benefit of freshness and by relating freshness to Green Giant. Retrieval of any attribute facilitates activating the others as well as the freshness benefit. Each advertising spot is linked to the others in the campaign by ensuring that all spots share a common context (i.e., the valley), and by selecting attributes that all suggest Green Giant means freshness.

A variant on the Big Idea, which we call the Big Idea II, involves the introduction of an attribute or reason to believe to generate an associative network (figure 9.1). Here, the goal is to develop the campaign around the different functional benefits implied by an attribute. For example, consider a tire system that monitors the air pressure in each tire and reports the results to the driver via a dashboard indicator. In addition, the tire runs flat without doing damage for 50 miles. These attributes imply that low air pressure can be detected quickly and thus increase the driver's safety as well as improve gas economy. The run-flat feature also suggests the benefit of not needing a spare tire, which would offer more useable trunk space and increase gas mileage. By presenting the safety, economy, and space implications, an associative network is built to facilitate recall of the benefits related to the monitoring and run flat attributes when making a tire decision. Amplification using the Big Idea strategies is presented in figure 9.1.

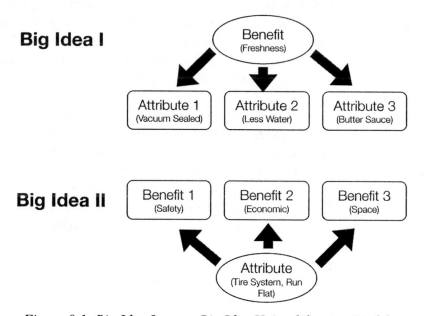

Figure 9.1: Big Idea I versus Big Idea II Amplification Models

Story Grammar

The story grammar approach was popularized by Doyle, Dane & Bernbach (now DDB Needham) in the 1960s and is commonly used in advertising today. It is based on the notion that people store information in memory using the following structure: problem (or opportunity), episodes to address the problem, and outcomes (figure 9.2). From an early age, children exhibit the ability to process information that is presented in a problem-episode-outcome story grammar format as manifested by their understanding of fairy tales and nursery rhymes. Advertising messages take advantage of this structure by showing the problem that the brand solves and then detailing the step-by-step process by which it creates a successful outcome. In DDB's version of story grammar, the brand is shown solving extreme problems with the notion that if the brand could manage this extremely challenging situation, it would work well in the less challenging contexts typically faced by consumers. For example, Pepto-Bismol recently introduced an ad campaign utilizing story grammar. In these ads, concerned callers are humorously depicted detailing their gastrointestinal dilemmas to a Pepto-Bismol hotline operator who gives tips on how to alleviate these stomach problems. The advice solves the problem.

Story Grammar

Figure 9.2: Elements of a Story Grammar

Perhaps the best-known illustration of DDB's story grammar approach is the introductory campaign for VW in the early 1960s. The commercial opens by showing the person who drives the snowplow driving through a snowstorm to the snowplow in a Volkswagen. The problem is getting to the snowplow, the episodes are challenges faced by the VW owner making it through the snow, and the solution is the VW owner driving away in the snowplow. Linkage of the benefit to the brand name is achieved by making the brand the hero and the solution to the problem.

In some cases, the story grammar is extended over time so that each ad becomes part of a serial presentation. One such example from the early 1990s is a series of mini-drama ads by Nestle promoting its Gold Blend brand in the UK, and its Taster's Choice brand of instant coffee in the US. The ads followed the paths of two amorous neighbors, Tony and Sharon, whose relationship slowly developed over many cups of instant coffee. This love story was of such interest to consumers that it later inspired a novel titled *Love Over Gold*. The campaign initially increased Taster's Choice share of the instant coffee market by 10%. But as the serial continued, consumers became more interested in the developing relationship between Tony and Sharon than the coffee, for which the ads were no longer providing news.

A story grammar can also be used effectively when a brand has no point of difference. As we discussed in **Chapter 5** on brand positioning, in such situations insight about the category serves as the point of difference. This strategy can be executed by illustrating the problem that consumers face, and then showing it solved by the advertised brand, without providing a reason to believe. Along these lines, Lee jeans showed the lengths people had to go to in an effort to get into most brands of jeans. Lee was presented as the solution to this problem. No rationale was provided to foster a belief in Lee's claim. Yet the campaign was effective because people felt that if Lee understood the difficulty they had buying jeans, Lee was likely to make ones that solved the problem of poor fit.

When using a story grammar approach to amplification, care is needed in deciding how much brand information to present. Often story grammars present substantial amounts of information by having the consumer facing the problem describe the brand's benefits. This approach is not effective if the audience perceives either that most consumers would not have such information, or even if they did, would not share it in the context shown. When this occurs, the verisimilitude of the story grammar is compromised; that is, what is shown happening is not the way it would really happen in an actual situation. Story grammar that lacks verisimilitude prompts message recipients to think about the fact that the scenario is not real rather than about the content of the advertising. For example, in an ad for a tooth whitening product, a couple is shown coming into a restaurant, where the host says "Welcome, I see you would like to be seated in the non-smoking section of the restaurant." The couple objects and say "But we smoke," as a way to suggesting how well the brand performs. The problem is that this exchange would never happen in real life, that is, it lacks verisimilitude. Those seeing such an ad typically think about how unrealistic the ad is rather than processing the information about the benefit.

Comparative Advertising

Comparative advertising involves pitting the attributes or benefits of a firm's brand against those of competitors' brands. Such comparison typically prompts amplification of the attributes or benefits compared in the ad. At the same time, critics of this approach express the concern that comparative advertising is free advertising for competitors. There is also the possibility that disparaging rival brands will lead consumers to think "let there be a pox on all of your brands."

Comparative advertising can be advantageous when a firm does not have the leading brand. Using comparison establishes a follower brand as a member of the same category as a leading brand. But if a follower brand is to invite comparison, it must offer demonstrable superiority on some characteristic that is important to consumers. The "Pepsi Challenge," where consumers were encouraged to compare the brand to its rival Coke, offers an example of effective use of comparison advertising. In market-by-market, Pepsi advertising demonstrating the brand's superiority in taste to that of Coke resulted in an increase in Pepsi's market share.

A leading brand in a category typically would not compare itself to the competition. The leading brand is already closely associated with the product category, so such a comparison would be unlikely to enhance brand membership in the category. Identifying competition might also legitimize competitive brands that consumers may not have previously considered as viable alternatives. For the leading brand, comparative advertising might be free advertising for a competitor. Why, then, would a leading brand ever compare itself with the competition? This tends to occur when the comparison offers a more powerful way to show superiority on some benefit than is possible by simply presenting the merits of the advertised brand. Thus, it is appropriate for a market leader to use comparison when they believe that the increased power of a comparison offsets the potential liabilities of enhancing a competitor's membership in the category. And, in many categories consumers know the follower brand, so identifying the brand in advertising provides no news.

Leading brands can also make effective use of comparison by using the brand's own previous performance as a comparison standard. Duracell, the leader in the battery category, compares its new battery to its previous one as a means of delivering news.

Analogies

Analogies are commonly used advertising devices that foster the amplification of a brand benefit by relating it to some other object or concept that is known to consumers. They are particularly popular when the task involves the promotion of services and other abstract entities. Analogies involve the transfer of internal knowledge from a base that is known by the message recipient to a target that is being learned with the goal of facilitating the learning of the target. For example, the assertion that Palm Pilot is a secretary enables people who understand a secretary's function (base) to transfer this knowledge and gain an understanding of how a Palm Pilot might function (target). In the process, a feature that might not otherwise be salient becomes focal to the audience.

Several precautions are warranted in using analogies. First, expertise in the base is required if message recipients are to be able to map relationships in their memory from the base to a target. In addition, substantial resources are needed to perform such a mapping. And the difficulty of this task is often exacerbated by the presence of competitors who are also using an analogy to highlight their brand's point of difference. For example, casual inspection of ad pages within *Fortune*, *Business Week* or other business publications, where many consulting services advertise their brands, reveals that most of these advertisers use a metaphor to talk about their brands' benefits. For example, golf pro Tiger Woods is the spokesperson for the consulting firm Accenture and ads frequently employ golf analogies such as "Why high performers shine even when the sun doesn't" using Tiger's superior performance on a rainy day as an analogy to a client's ability to perform when economic conditions are similarly bleak with the help of Accenture's services. Deloitte Consulting portrays its client as a ringmaster, where with the help of Deloitte, he or she can now restore order amidst chaos.

This practice raises the possibility that the reader will be overwhelmed by the processing/cognitive demands of these ads if they are to be processed in detail. In addition, the use of the same persuasive device by several advertisers, and especially by brands in the same category, limits the persuasive impact of a message in the same way as occurs when brands do not articulate substantive points of difference. In both instances the lack of brand differentiation undermines the linkage of the ad to the brand.

In other situations, analogies fail to persuade because they are not used appropriately. Most often this occurs because attention centers on the base rather than having message recipients use the base to understand the target. For example, EDS, an information technology outsourcing firm, aired a commercial where they describe their role in helping their customers by using an analogy to herding cats. The advertising then detailed the difficulties in herding cats with the idea that people seeing the message would conclude that EDS helps organize even unruly clients. The problem with this use of analogy is that the herding cats base was unknown, and thus had to be learned. This required that the message recipient abandon the effort to map the base into the target services offered by EDS as the consumer must first understand the base to establish its connections to the target. In most cases, consumers do not have the motivation to work through such an analogy in the detail needed to understand the brand's point of difference.

Spokespeople as Prompts for Message Amplification

Amplification of a brand's position in an advertising message can also be achieved by having spokespeople deliver a persuasive appeal. Spokespeople are typically characterized along three dimensions: attractiveness, expertise and trustworthiness. Attractive spokespeople are not difficult to find; celebrities serve this purpose. Experts too are available. Anyone who has detailed knowledge about the category and brand can serve as an expert. This includes CEOs and others who work at the sponsoring firm and consumers who have substantial experience with a category. More difficult to identify are those who are perceived as trustworthy, that is, those who are perceived as motivated to share their knowledge in an accurate manner. Consumers understand that spokespeople are paid for their advocacy, and this knowledge undermines the trustworthiness of most spokespeople. We examine the virtues and liabilities of using spokespeople, as well as strategies to address the limitations of their use.

Use of Attractive Spokespeople

In some instances, spokespeople are selected because they are attractive; that is, they are dynamic, likable, or of high status. Joe Montana served as a spokesperson for TiVo, and Catherine Zeta Jones promoted the T-Mobile brand. Such attractive people are typically chosen as spokespeople because their presence enhances advertising recall. However, in assessing this strategy, it is important to examine what is recalled when a celebrity spokesperson is the brand advocate. Often it is associations to the celebrity rather than recall of the brand information presented in the message. The result is that the impact of advertising is modest.

This observation does not imply that celebrity spokespeople should not be used. They can be effective if their attributes of character can be used to personify the brand's benefit. Tiger Woods is an appropriate spokesperson for Nike because he personifies Nike's commitment to performance and aspiration to greatness. Similarly, the endorsement of Max Factor cosmetics by Gisele Bundchen, the famous Brazilian model, is a means of conveying the idea that this brand offers cutting edge products for hip young women. Thus, using a spokesperson to personify the brand benefit provides another cue to amplify consumers' associations to the brand.

Expert and Trustworthy Spokespeople

There is substantial evidence that personification is not the only means by which spokespeople influence amplification. Those who are credible by virtue of their knowledge about a brand or category (i.e., experts) and who are motivated to share this knowledge (i.e., trustworthy) can influence amplification by reducing consumers' motivation to retrieve their own thoughts about a message advocacy that they would otherwise consider. In contrast, less expert and trustworthy spokespeople prompt consumers to activate their own repertoire of thoughts in response to a message.

These observations imply that an expert and trustworthy spokesperson is valuable when people are opposed to the position taken in a message. This follows from the finding that such sources reduce retrieval of thoughts, which in this instance would be negative thoughts or counterarguments to the message. Thus, the presence of trustworthy and expert spokespeople enhances the impact of messages that run counter to the attitude held by message recipients. However, when people favor a message advocacy, as they might if they were users of a brand, spokespeople who are not known for their trustworthiness and expertise would be more persuasive than those with greater credibility on these dimensions because they would stimulate the activation of consumers' own thoughts, which would be favorable to the brand in this instance. This observation does not give the strategist license to use the least trustworthy and expert spokesperson available when advertising to those favorable to a brand. To do so might undermine influence. Rather, the implication is that using a spokesperson in these circumstances is not warranted.

These observations imply that when consumers do not have favorable attitudes toward a brand, a spokesperson is an asset by prompting consumers to suppress their negative thoughts and use their available cognitive resources to process the arguments presented in the ad. Conversely, the expense of hiring a spokesperson is not necessary if the advertising is directed at consumers who already have favorable brand attitudes. In this situation, having free cognitive resources works in the advertiser's favor as consumers utilizes available resources in the retrieval of preexisting positive brand information they have stored in long-term memory.

Although it is evident that trustworthiness and expertise can influence amplification, as we noted earlier, it is difficult to apply this knowledge in advertising because spokespeople are not typically perceived to be trustworthy. One way to overcome this problem is to use spokespeople whose integrity is unquestionable. For example, British Telecom used theoretical physicist Stephen Hawking to support the proposition that communication could be used to better the world. In some countries, expert sources are so revered that their use has been regulated. Along these lines, healthcare professionals and celebrities in China have been banned from appearing in advertisements for drugs or nutritional supplements.

Risks in Using Spokespeople

Regardless, of the goal in using spokespeople, it is important to recognize that spokespeople's behavior can damage the brand. This might occur if spokespeople engage in some behavior that is embarrassing to the brand and thus *destroys* the spokesperson's ability to personify the brand's benefit. Ben Curtis, who became well known for saying "You're getting a Dell Dude," was caught with drugs and therefore personified something with which Dell did not want to be associated. When a spokesperson becomes popular, there is an increased possibility of *dilution* of the brand. For example, after John Gilchrist portrayed a young boy named Mikey, who was a picky eater, became a successful spokesperson for Life cereal, he was subsequently hired to endorse Pepto Bismol, Jell-O and Skippy peanut butter. Although Mikey was shown liking these brands, none experienced the same lift in business as Life. Mikey's overexposure diluted his impact. Successful spokespeople often realize that they are an important part of a brand's equity and threaten to *defect* when their contract demands are not met. Jared Fogle, who lost 245 pounds on a Subway diet, quit as spokesperson in a disagreement with the brand, but was rehired when Subway sales dropped 10%.

In some cases, spokespeople have little connection to the brand, but are salient in their own right, which results in *distracting* consumers from the brand message. Taco Bell used a Chihuahua as the spokesperson for the brand. While consumers loved the dog, this spokesperson did not enhance sales. In fact, during the Chihuahua campaign, Taco Bell sales fell 10%. Spokespeople, and particularly older ones, raise the possibility of *death* during a campaign. Death of a spokesperson typically results in the advertising being pulled and the development of a new campaign, which is both expensive and time consuming. Great Western Bank ads starring actor John Wayne were pulled when the legendary actor died, and US West stopped airing its Yellow Pages advertising when famous chef James Beard died. Finally, spokespeople can be *dominated* by competitors using more compelling sources, especially if these spokespeople share the same expertise. Although Larry Bird was a credible spokesperson for Converse, his effectiveness was diminished by Nike's use of Michael Jordan as their spokesperson. Thus, despite the fact that spokespeople can be powerful instruments of message persuasion, there are six dangers that require consideration when the use of a spokesperson is contemplated. They can destroy, dilute, defect, distract, die or be dominated by another spokesperson. We refer to these as the Six Deadly Ds.

Overcoming Spokesperson Liabilities

A question that can be raised is whether the benefits of spokespeople can be tapped without the associated risks? One approach to temper the degree of risk is for a brand to use multiple spokespeople. When a brand has multiple spokespeople, it is easier to shift attention away from the misbehavior of a single spokesperson. Of course, the cost of this strategy limits its use to advertisers with large budgets.

A less expensive approach is to use testimonials from consumers. Testimonials can have great impact when the spokesperson is someone like the target audience but more experienced with the category than the audience. Moms with several kids under the age of six are persuasive spokespeople for products such as diapers and infant formula.

Finally, to address both the cost and concerns about spokespeople, a growing number of firms are using iconography in lieu of spokespeople for their brands. Examples include the Aflac duck, the Geico gecko, M&M candies, and Erin Esurance. Although such characters often do not have the same status as celebrities or experts, they offer a viable way to promote amplification without the risks attendant to using attractive, expert and trustworthy sources.

Background Factors Influencing Message Amplification

The factors that influence amplification of a message advocacy that we have examined to this point are focal elements of the persuasive messages themselves. However, advertising also includes background elements to stimulate amplification of a brand's position. We examine the role of two of these elements, music and color.

Music

The use of music is common in advertising. Often the music used in advertising is upbeat and pleasant. This practice seems justified by research indicating that a positive mood can both foster persuasion and serve as an impetus to make connections among disparate objects. One such application involves the processing of analogies, which require the message recipient to see the connection between a base and a target as previously discussed. It has been found that upbeat music creates a positive feeling that enhances the persuasive impact of an analogy among those with limited knowledge of the base category. This music had no effect on those with substantial knowledge, presumably because their expertise enabled them to see the connection between base and target in the absence of music. A more detailed analysis of the effect of mood is provided by Lee and Sternthal (1999), and Roehm and Sternthal, (2001).

Featuring music in advertising can be used to focus consumers' attention towards particular aspects of a message. This might entail varying the loudness or the pitch of the music at certain points in the visual presentation or setting the execution to particular moments of the song (e.g., the chorus). The use of music for such purposes is particularly useful when message recipients would otherwise not be attentive to the message content. In contrast, for those who are highly involved in learning the message content, musical devices can distract attention from amplifying on the message content.

When music is used as an integral part of the advertising appeal, lyrics promoting the features of the product are sung to music. For example, in promoting its Big Mac sandwich, McDonald's ran commercials that described the ingredients in a catchy song: "Two all beef patties, special sauce, lettuce, cheese, pickles, onions on a sesame seed bun." The processing of these elements, as well as the fact that the music itself might convey meaning relevant to the brand, generally makes apprehending advertising that includes music complex and effortful to process. This complexity makes music the choice of advertisers who are concerned about wearout. The assumption is that because the message is complex, recipients will continue to learn from the message even after a substantial number of exposures to it. Thus, fast food outlets, soft drinks and other products and services that spend heavily on advertising tend to use musical appeals. Music is also used frequently in radio advertising where wearout is likely by virtue of the frequency delivered by the medium. In circumstances where music is used to enhance the amplification of the brand benefit, but the ad budget is limited, devices are used to increase the ease with which the music is processed. For example, a hook can be used where the brand's point of difference is read dramatically just prior to the musical appeal as a means of facilitating message processing ("now Mountain Dew is smoother than smooth").

Color

Color can be an effective means of prompting message recipients to amplify their feelings about the product or the context of use. Red implies active and lively, blue suggests cool and serene, and yellow is associated with medicinal and weak. Pastels imply a product is feminine, whereas dark colors and especially dark brown imply masculinity. The use of white lettering on a black background suggests the product is high tech. The use of black and white in advertising is associated with retro. And the use of substantial white space in print advertising is a means of communicating purity or simplicity. When the VW Beetle was first introduced a small visual of the car was shown on a white page as a means of emphasizing its point of difference, which was its small size.

One issue in using color presentations is that they are typically more resource demanding to process than black and white presentations. This property can undermine persuasion when resources are limited. In this circumstance, message recipients might use their cognitive resources to process the meaning of the color rather than the persuasive content of the message. When complex verbal information is to be transmitted, consideration should be given to using black and white advertising.

Color can also be used to direct attention. Advertisers use color highlighting to have the audience focus on the product or some other element that is critical to the persuasiveness of the message. Thus, 7UP used a black and white ad in which the bottle of 7UP was in red to emphasize that the brand came in a cherry flavor. A more detailed discussion of color effects is provided in Meyers-Levy and Peracchio (1995).

Prompting Audience-Based Amplification: Sexual Innuendo

Amplification can be triggered primarily by message content or it can rely primarily on consumers' associations. Sexual innuendo illustrates the latter approach to amplification. This approach is often justified on the basis of Freudian psychodynamics. According to this view, individuals pass through several stages of development in early life. At each stage, the individual must overcome frustrations and anxieties. One argument for using sexual cues in advertising is that it provides a means for consumers to deal with unresolved frustrations. Sexual innuendo is proposed to allow people to discharge tensions in a relatively harmless way perhaps even without their knowledge due to the subliminal or subtle nature of these cues. Further, because people have many associations to their sexual frustrations, message information is likely to be easily related to information previously stored in memory. A second argument for sexual innuendo is that it might serve as a form of "subliminal persuasion." Because consumers might not readily detect the innuendo they might be more open to persuasion. Consistent with the notion of sexual innuendo, advertising for cigarettes often uses phallic cues such a pogo sticks, pool cues and the like, which resonates with smokers' concerns about their potency.

Providing the Resources for Message Amplification

Amplification is a resource demanding task. A variety of strategies are employed to provide the resources individuals require to amplify on a message. As we discussed in our analysis of media strategy, repetition of a message can be used for this purpose. Here, we examine the use of two devices to activate resources needed for amplification, fear and humor.

Fear Appeals

From every day experience, it might be expected that inducing emotions related to fear or threat would be an effective means of motivation. Admonitions to children such as "don't touch the hot stove or you will be burned" seem to be influential without repetition. However, in formal inquiry pertaining to threat appeals, it has been found that threat need not stimulate persuasion, and might even undermine it.

Theorizing about the impact of fear appeals provides a basis for understanding when they are likely to be effective and when they might undermine the persuasive impact of a message. According to this theorizing, threatening information can be processed by one of two systems that operate in parallel. The system that is operative depends on the type of advertising information presented. One system is called *danger control*. As figure 9.3 shows, the danger control system processes information regarding what constitutes danger, who is in danger, and how to control danger. This information is stored in memory and can stimulate actions that are adaptive in coping with danger with the intention of eliminating danger or reducing the perceived threat through practical action.

The other system is *fear control*. Fear control involves the processing of information about the dire consequences of noncompliance with the message advocacy. This method produces an emotional response that consumers seek to alleviate by introducing habitual and idiosyncratic means of dealing with fear. These actions are not necessarily aimed at reducing the threat, but instead are individual coping mechanisms for dealing with the fear induced by the message. For some people, this entails coping with fear by sleeping, for others it involves eating and for still others it prompts smoking.

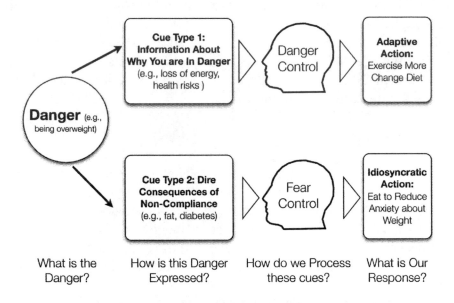

Figure 9.3: The Effect of Fear Appeals: Danger Control and Fear Control

To clarify the implications of this view, consider a commercial advocating that people should stop smoking. If the advertiser's intention is to induce adaptive action, the audience should be told about what constitutes danger with regard to smoking. Operationally, this might involve telling people that there is danger if they have a hacking cough, or cannot walk up a flight of stairs without getting short of breath. In addition, adaptive action may be stimulated by recommending ways of coping with danger. This might include recommendations such as placing cigarettes in inconvenient locations and drawing a circle around the middle of the cigarettes and only smoking them down to that line. By contrast, one would avoid showing gory illustrations of smokers' blackened lungs, or stating dire consequences such as "Be sure you have a lot of insurance; your kids will need it to go to college." Focusing on dire consequences might trigger fear, and thus induce an emotional response. This response might not be adaptive. Some people might even light up a cigarette as a means of coping with the fear induced.

The foregoing analysis suggests that inducing fear per se is an inappropriate strategy for persuasion. So-called threatening appeals should focus on helping people to recognize danger and how to cope with it. This type of information is likely to be used in pursuing an adaptive course of action. Although it may not be possible to eliminate all mention of the dire consequences of noncompliance, information about consequences should be relegated to the background. Otherwise, it is likely to stimulate individuals' own repertoire of thoughts, which may or may not lead to adaptive action.

Humorous Appeals

Some form of inducing audience emotions related to humor is used in more than half of commercials aired on television. Advertisers use turns-of-phrase, double entendre, slapstick and the like to stimulate message processing. The available evidence suggests that humor is an effective device for gaining attention and motivating an audience to amplify on the message information. However, it is equally evident that humor is not always an effective means of persuading consumers to consider a brand. In some cases, it might undermine this outcome.

Several guidelines might be followed by advertisers to enhance the persuasiveness of humorous appeals. Most important is that the humor prompts message recipients to focus on the brand's point of difference. Humor motivates consumers to attend to information related to the humor. If this information is brand-related, humor can foster amplification of this information. If, however, the humor is not related to the brand, humor can distract from processing message content.

A second guideline is that humor should be focused on the product and not the user. Making the product user the brunt of the joke might stimulate counterarguments and thus limit persuasion. If it is not feasible to focus humor on the product, it is preferable to make nonusers of the product rather than its users the brunt of the humor. This approach is illustrated by an Argentinean ad for Dr. Scholl's. A fisherman is shown sitting on a dock with his feet in the water. Before he can cast, the fish come to the surface, apparently dead from his foot odor. The remedy is Dr. Scholl's foot powder. Alternatively, one can make the product benefit the source of the humor. The VW Beetle was introduced to the US as an ugly little bug, but those who purchased it were described as smart and economical.

Third, when using humor, multiple advertisements are often required. Because humor stimulates attention, repeated exposure to the same humorous appeal quickly causes wearout because message recipients have already assimilated the news. For example, Nestle utilized humor featuring Bart Simpson in several of its Butterfinger ads where the context in which Bart stopped people from eating his Butterfingers changed from ad to ad ("Nobody better lay a finger on my Butterfinger"), but the same crispy, crunchy, peanut-buttery benefit was presented in all of the ads. This approach has the potential for wearout. To combat wearout, different benefits across executions are often needed to sustain brand news.

Critics of using humor in advertising are not satisfied by the application of these guidelines. They argue that humor usurps time that could be better spent informing people about a product's virtues. Although it is undoubtedly true that some factual information must be sacrificed in favor of humor, it should be noted that there is nothing inherent in a humorous approach to require substantial time for its development. For example, in a commercial where the goal was to inform consumers that a bank was offering promotions such as free karate lessons, they showed a women in her 70s as a voice over said her name and then said "free karate lessons?" with a laugh. The woman responded with a karate chop. This 15 second humorous spot resulted in a huge increase in bank deposits.

Summary of Creative Strategy

The persuasive impact of a message can be enhanced by stimulating recipients to amplify on the message. In this chapter we have discussed a number of strategies that might serve this purpose (e.g., hard sell, big idea, story grammar, analogies, spokespeople, music, color) and we have enumerated several approaches to providing the resources to consumers in order for them to amplify the message (Threat and humor). These strategies, as well as a description of when to use them and potential liabilities, are summarized in table 9.1.

Amplification Device	When to Use	Potential Liabilities
Hard Sell/Soft Sell (buy this brand get this benefit)	Brand has an important point of differences	Does not work if strong point of difference absent
Big Idea I (Attributes associated with a benefit)	Have a benefit with many attributes	Lack of brand linkage
Big Idea II (Benefits associated with an attribute)	Have an attribute that implies many benefits	Lack of brand linkage: Use multiple cues to ensure linkage
Story Grammar (Problem-Episode-Outcome)	When demonstration of the benefit is important	Lack of brand linkage Lack of verisimilitude
Analogies (Relating a known base to an unknown product)	How a brand works is difficult to convey	Resource demanding Ineffective if base is unfamiliar
Spokespeople (attractive, expert, trustworthy)	Personification when other ways of amplifying benefit not available	Six Deadly D's: destroys, dilutes, defects, distracts, dies, dominated
Music	To support brand-related emotion and focus attention	Can distract resources away from message amplification
Color	Another cue to prompt amplification	Resource demanding
Threat	Can foster danger control	Need to avoid fear control
Humor	When resources needed to process message content	Humor undermines ad when not focused on the brand benefit or nonuser

Table 9.1: Summary of Amplification and Resource Strategies

Chapter Exercises

• Pick at a current advertisement. Can you identify what cr-eative strategies from table 9.1 are present in the execution? Are the cre-ative strategies identified executed in an appropriate fashion? What other strategies might be employed in the next execution by the brand?

• Consider the use of fear and humor in advertising. Identify a recent execution that effectively or ineffectively users fear or humor. Explain the appropriateness of the strategy as used in the execution and, if problematic, the problem with the execution.

• Consider the following scenario. A computer company has a new graphics card. One way to use this news is to build a campaign about several benefits offered by this graphics card (e.g., able to run applications in higher quality, able to run applications faster, able to run more applications simultaneously). Alternatively, they could use the graphics card as a reason to believe the superior functionality of their machines. Identify the creative strategies that are being considered by the brand. What are the virtues and liabilities of each of these proposed creative strategies?

Recommended Readings

Lee, Angela Y., and Brian Sternthal (1999), "The Effects of Positive Mood on Memory," *Journal of Consumer Research*, 26, 115-127.

Meyers-Levy, Joan and Laura Peracchio (1995), "Understanding the Effects of Color: How the Correspondence between Available and Required Resources Affects Attitudes," *Journal of Consumer Research* (September), *22, 121-138.*

Roehm, Michelle L. and Brian Sternthal (2001), "The Moderating Effect of Knowledge and Resources on the Persuasive Impact of Analogies," *Journal of Consumer Research*, 28, 257-272.

Rucker, Derek D., and Adam D. Galinsky (2009), "Conspicuous Consumption versus Utilitarian Ideals: How Different Levels of Power Shape Consumer Behavior," *Journal of Experimental Social Psychology*, 45, 549-555.

Rucker, Derek D., Richard E. Petty, Joseph R. Priester (2007), "Understanding advertising effectiveness from a psychological perspective: The importance of attitudes and attitude strength." In Gerard J. Tellis and Tim Ambler (Editors), *The Handbook of Advertising* (pp. 71-88). Thousand Oaks, CA: Sage.

Chapter 10 Objectives

- ADPLAN: Attention, Distinctiveness, Positioning, Linkage, Amplification, Net Equity
- Advertiser-agency relations

Karen Black was thinking about the creative pitch she had just been given. The agency had mocked up a print ad for the new Volkswagen Passat 2.0 that they were recommending for the print campaign, but also as the basis for the TV advertising that had yet to be developed. Using a print idea to motivate the TV spot was standard practice at many firms because print made it easy to focus on whether the key advertising idea was compelling or not. Karen was pleased with the mock print ad. The print ad featured a picture of a white four door Volkswagen Passat 2.0 with chrome wire hub caps that was shown on a powder blue background that took up the top two-thirds of the page. Beneath this visual was the headline "**Boat**" in bold letters. The copy shown in figure 10.1 and the VW logo were presented beneath the picture of the car and the Boat headline. But she was hesitant to give the go ahead to develop TV advertising without further analysis of this ad because $36 million in TV, print and Internet media spending was on the line. Before taking the next step, it seemed worthwhile to review the strategy and the execution represented by the print ad in a systematic way.

Some misperceptions take time to die.

This one will take less than seven seconds.

That's how long the Volkswagen Passat 2.0 takes to reach 60 mph.

Faster than the BMW 525i, Lexus LS 250, and Mercedes C 230!

And yet it manages to best them all in fuel efficiency as well--delivering up to 6 mpg or more!

Not your typical luxury liner. Although it does offer a boatload of performance features like four corner suspension, push button ignition, and the Electronic Stabilization Program.

But what's most surprising is that even with better fuel efficiency and more torque than those other cars, the Passat costs about $10,000 less.

How's it possible? Simple. It's a Volkswagen.

When you think of all the facts and all the awards its won, the argument that you have to pay a lot of money for a performance car just doesn't hold water. And at just $23,180, it's another reason why when you get into a Volkswagen, it gets into you.

Figure 10.1: Copy from Print Execution for Volkswagen Passat 2.0

In this chapter, we suggest an approach to assessing advertising either prior to engaging in testing research or in lieu of it. We refer to this approach using the acronym ADPLAN. This approach reflects the considerations that underlie the advertising evaluations made by many firms. ADPLAN prompts an assessment of both the strategy and the creative execution.

The ADPLAN Framework

ADPLAN identifies six factors that warrant consideration in evaluating advertising. Many elements of ADPLAN have been discussed or alluded to previously in our analysis of brand positioning as well as media and creative strategy. Here, we discuss these elements as a means of evaluating the likely effectiveness of advertising such as that developed for the VW Passat 2.0. Examined first is the question of whether the creative execution captures and holds *attention*. Second, is the style of the execution such that there is *distinctiveness* from executions developed by other brands in competing as well as unrelated categories? Third, does the execution present the desired *positioning* in terms of both the frame of reference and the point of difference in a clear fashion? Fourth, is there strong *linkage* between the brand and benefit promoted in the ad? Fifth, is the advertising likely to prompt positive *amplification* of the message information? Finally, does the execution fit with the *net equity* of the brand in terms of style and substance? These six criteria compose *ADPLAN* (figure 10.2). A truly effective advertisement will typically address all of the questions posed in figure 10.1 affirmatively, at least to some degree, whereas a poor execution will often significantly fail on one or more of the questions. Each criterion is discussed in detail.

Attention

Attention is a critical element in designing advertising. Copy writers' and art directors' first concern in developing an ad is to make sure it breaks through the boredom barrier. To assess this issue, it is important to assess whether the ad captures people's attention.

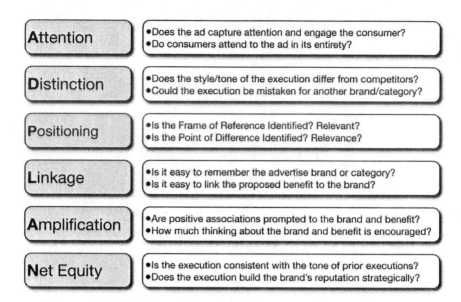

Attention	•Does the ad capture attention and engage the consumer? •Do consumers attend to the ad in its entirety?
Distinction	•Does the style/tone of the execution differ from competitors? •Could the execution be mistaken for another brand/category?
Positioning	•Is the Frame of Reference Identified? Relevant? •Is the Point of Difference Identified? Relevance?
Linkage	•Is it easy to remember the advertise brand or category? •Is it easy to link the proposed benefit to the brand?
Amplification	•Are positive associations prompted to the brand and benefit? •How much thinking about the brand and benefit is encouraged?
Net Equity	•Is the execution consistent with the tone of prior executions? •Does the execution build the brand's reputation strategically?

Figure 10.2: ADPLAN Evaluation Criteria

One element that induces attention is incongruity. The VW ad draws attention by its headline "Boat." This is inconsistent with the audience's expectation because boat is a pejorative way to describe a car; it implies that it is a large, difficult to maneuver, gas-guzzler. And it runs afoul of the heritage of VW in the US, which was a producer of small cars. Attention can be sustained by the inclusion of news, which VW does by telling people about the performance and economy that is delivered by the Passat 2.0. The media context in which the advertising appears can also affect attention to the ad. Ads featured during the Superbowl tend to receive more consumer attention given their high production values; however, this greater attention does not guarantee memory for the brand or the ad. Alternatively, media can draw attention by their resonance with customers' moment and mindset. Along these lines, the Passat advertising might be presented on Edmunds.com website that reviews auto performance, or on search websites such as Google for targeted customers who have previously visited BMW, Lexus and Mercedes sites. Further, because these sites allow for self-paced information presentations, consumers will have the time to process detailed information that has caught their eye. To assess whether attention is attracted, consumers are asked to recall information about the brand, which is compared to the information presented in advertising.

Distinctiveness

Distinctiveness refers to whether the tone and manner of the execution distinguishes the advertising from other executions, and particularly ones in the same category. Ads strong on this dimension are unique and not easily mistaken for another type of execution, whereas ads weak on the distinctiveness dimension could easily have been for another brand in the same or a different category. The VW Passat ad has limited distinctiveness, which occurs in the headline "Boat." This headline is unlike the ones used in the category. At the same time, the product visual is similar to many other car ads. In contrast, ads for iPhone are distinctive in their execution. The product fills the ad space and the copy is sparse. Even a quick glance at the ad and the brand is recognized.

What are the benefits of strong distinctiveness? Distinctiveness is a basis for attracting attention. Tellabs, a telecommunications provider for companies that market services in this category, presented a print campaign featuring animals and nature scenes to motivate the discussion of its benefits. For example, owls were used when the feature was the vigilance with which Tellabs equipment monitors its customers' networks, and goats served as the visual when discussing the scalability of Tellabs' equipment. Because the campaign was published in technology oriented magazines, where executions are technically oriented, the Tellabs executions were highly distinctive. Not only were these ads noticed, they were the topic of discussion within firms that purchased telecommunications products. In addition, when distinctiveness is sustained over time, it enhances brand linkage. Six flags dancing mascot, Mr. Six (a.k.a. "the Ambassador of Fun") instantly relates the brand to having fun, and Charles Schwab animated people help to distinguish the brand from a host of brokerage ads that feature sixties music, boomers sailing and relaxing on Adirondack chairs.

One way to assess distinctiveness is to develop mock ads. Consumers are shown the Passat ad anew, but this time the brand name is omitted. They are asked to indicate the brand that is being advertised. Or they can be shown the Passat ad with the brand name replaced by another brand and asked whether they saw this ad or not. The percent of those who report the correct response to these questions provides an indication of the ad's distinctiveness. A discussion of potential threats to the distinctiveness of an execution is offered by Kent and Allen (1994).

Positioning

It is often not sufficient to develop advertising that holds attention and has distinctiveness in the hope of later relating it to the brand. If advertising is to be effective, it must often make the connection to the brand's position from the outset. Otherwise, consumers are invited to develop their own views of what the brand represents. Thus, evaluating the effectiveness of an ad requires a consideration of how well the brand's position is represented in the advertising: is the brand's frame of reference and point of difference presented effectively in the creative execution?

In the Passat ad, it is immediately evident that the frame is a car. This is achieved by the visual of the brand and the VW logo. The frame of reference is refined by placing the Passat in a luxury car frame of reference. This involves naming of BMW, Lexus, and Mercedes as the brands against which Passat competes. The copy also delivers the value point of difference: greater performance at a lower purchase price and maintenance cost. The value proposition is supported by reasons to believe. The price of the Passat is listed, as is the savings that this price represents. The greater fuel economy is also supported by factual information.

It should be noted that in assessing the position an assumption is made that the positioning is appropriate for the target. The evaluation task does not involve revisiting the adequacy of the position, but rather determining whether the frame of reference and point of difference are delivered in the creative execution. In the VW Passat ad, it might be argued that consumers will not be convinced that VW is a member of the luxury frame of reference, and there is the possibility that this frame of reference will be perceived as inconsistent with the VW claim of greater fuel economy.

To measure whether the position has been executed effectively, three questions might be posed to consumers. A correct response to a brand awareness question (what is the VW Passat 2.0?) would offer evidence that the frame of reference has registered with consumers. And a correct response to a consideration set question (If you were planning to buy a luxury car, what brands would you consider purchasing?) would offer evidence that the Passat was viewed in the context of the luxury car category. Finally, to assess whether Passat's point of difference was processed and whether it was persuasive, consumers might be asked what features distinguish Passat from other luxury cars, and whether these features would prompt them to consider purchasing the Passat when they next planned a car purchase. Importantly if consumers indicate the advertised features are not compelling reasons to buy the car, this might be an indication of a poorly chosen brand position.

Linkage

A critical issue in evaluating advertising is the linkage between the brand name and the benefit claimed in advertising. If consumers do not associate the message with the brand name, advertising will be ineffective. Thus, executions that are strong on this dimension are ones where the category, brand, and benefit are easy for consumers to remember and relate to each other, whereas executions that are weak on this dimension leave the consumer unsure about the brand that sponsored the advertising. In the VW Passat ad, the question is whether consumers remember the superior value benefit and whether they attach it to Passat 2.0.

Factors that Undermine Linkage. One factor that can undermine the linkage to a brand in dynamic executions (e.g., television, radio, viral videos) is the late identification (late ID) of the brand name. By withholding the brand name until the end of the ad, the audience is invited to make its own associations. Audiences frequently associate the commercial with some other brand or category.

The rationale for using a late ID is that it serves as an engagement device. That is, the lack of brand identification builds suspense that leads consumers to attend to the execution. This rationale is justified if brand linkage is not compromised. For example, when Tums found that people often responded to their advertising by arguing that such a small tablet could not be as effective an antacid as Tums was claiming, a late ID was introduced. The commercial showed an extreme close-up of a green Tums tablet that was revolving slowly as its efficacy was being described. Only at the end of the commercial was the tablet in a position where the brand name could be read. This commercial not only halted brand erosion but resulted in a significant upturn in business. The late ID forestalled the audience's counterarguments until a point when it would have required consumers to expend great effort to activate their prior knowledge to offset what they had learned about Tums.

It should be noted that the difficulties posed by late ID is primarily an American phenomenon. In Europe, Asia and South America, late ID is frequently and effectively used in advertising. In these countries, advertising is often viewed more as entertainment than a means of obtaining brand information. Late IDs are a way of delivering entertainment. Late IDs are also effective because the total number of campaigns that are presented to consumers is much smaller than the number to which American consumers are exposed, and because each campaign is sustained for a much longer period of time than in the US. These factors make it relatively easy for those in countries other than the US to keep track of the benefit that a brand is advertising. These observations suggest that as the density of advertising in other countries increases, the same difficulty in using late IDs that is experienced in the U.S. is likely to surface elsewhere.

Another factor that can undermine brand linkage is walking away from a brand's equity. Brand name linkage to a benefit is often undermined when the advertising walks away from the brand's equity. Special K ready-to-eat cereal for many years promoted staying slim as its point of difference. When woman began to complain that this advertising promoted outdated values that marginalized women, a new campaign was aired featuring men complaining about their figures. While many consumers found this advertising entertaining, it had little linkage to Special K's positioning; sales fell dramatically and the campaign was retracted within a year. This suggests that when attempting to change the equity of the brand, special effort is required to sustain brand linkage.

Finally, brand name linkage to a benefit can be undermined by a lack of distinctiveness. For example, advertising for B.F. Goodrich has often been mistaken for Goodyear advertising. The fact that the names are similar and Goodyear did significantly more advertising undermined the linkage of Goodrich's advertising to the brand.

Enhancing Brand Linkage. How can the likelihood of brand linkage be enhanced? The brand name needs to be made prominent to consumers. This can be achieved by presenting the brand name early in message presentation and prior to the information about the benefit. In addition, it is useful to tie the brand to what people already know about it. When this is not possible, it is important to enhance its recall by creating associations to it in the message. For example, Cutty Sark is a brand of scotch drinkers associated with its tall sailing ship logo. When Cutty began to lose share, a campaign was developed that promoted brand recall and associated it to Cutty's heritage. It was "Don't give up the ship." Thus, for Father's Day the Cutty ad stated: "The best advice I ever got from my Daddy was... Don't give up the ship," and on New York subways the poster read "When you have had it up to here with graffiti, don't give up the ship." This slogan not only was memorable by virtue of the fact that it was the battle cry during the War of 1812, but also because it was closely linked to what consumers knew about the brand. The result was a resurgence of Cutty Sark's sales.

Finally, for some brands, linkage can be enhanced by sheer repetition of brand advertising. Brands with substantial ad budgets such as Geico and Budweiser have strong brand linkage because advertising is aired with great frequency.

Amplification

Executions that are strong on the dimension of amplification encourage the activation of associations to the message content and thus produce positive thoughts and evaluations (see Petty and Cacioppo 1979; Rucker and Petty 2006). The VW Passat ad prompts amplification by using comparison. Message recipients are encouraged to think about Passat's performance both in terms of power and economy in relation to other luxury cars. And they are invited to compare the cost of these alternatives. If consumers think about how Passat stacks up against luxury cars, the associations created are likely to make the message content accessible when they make a decision. In addition, the use of a powder blue back drop behind the car might imply authentic or basic, which is in keeping with VW's heritage but perhaps not its placement in a luxury car frame of reference. If advertising is deemed not to enhance amplification, the devices discussed in **Chapter 9** might be considered. These include: hard sell, big idea, story grammar, analogies, spokespeople, music and color.

In assessing amplification, consideration should be given about whether the associations generated will be positive or negative. It may be that the advertising provokes people to counterargue, in which case the brand evaluation will not be enhanced by the advertising. For example, in the Passat ad, people might acknowledge that the brand has a powerful engine and good gas economy, but the price quoted in the ad might lead them to discount the Passat because they believe that VW does not offer the same luxury or dealer service as the BMW, Lexus or Mercedes. Thus, advertising might prompt amplification in the form of negative associations, which would undermine ad effectiveness. If this problem is anticipated, it can be overcome by ensuring that the discrepancy between people's current beliefs and the brand promise is relatively small or by providing evidence that limits counterargumentation. The Passat advertising uses the latter approach to limit counterargumentation to its message.

Net Equity

Net equity refers to the degree to which an execution reflects the prior associations that consumers have to a brand. For example, BMW's equity is as the ultimate driving machine. Hallmark's equity is the best quality greeting card. An execution with strong net equity maintains or builds on the equity a brand has established or wishes to develop. An execution with poor net equity fails to reinforce or even walks away from the brand's equity. VW has equity in being economical, which is featured in the Passat ad, but placement of the brand in the luxury frame of reference might be viewed as a stretch by consumers. A detailed discussion of how to conceptualize, measure and manage equity is offered in Keller (1993).

It is easy for a brand to walk away from its equity. In an effort to get incremental volume, to react to consumer trends, or to respond to competition, brands often fail to support their equity. Tic Tac had equity as a powerful breath freshener. When it decided to target consumers who were concerned about their caloric intake by advertising that it had fewer calories than other breath fresheners, it invited other brands to promote fresher breath. The result was a steep decline in market share. Starbucks has equity as a special experience. This equity is not enhanced by the promotion of its new Pike's Place Roast coffee, which is less sophisticated and flavorful than its other offerings and aimed at appealing to the masses. Thus, any time a brand abandons its equity, it requires justification in terms of the magnitude of an alternative opportunity. In the vast majority of cases such justification is not available and a brand's advertising should be evaluated in terms of sustaining the net equity.

The key benefit of having strong equity is that the brand becomes synonymous with the benefit and thus serves as a barrier to competitive reactions. For example, Axe established its equity as the brand that attracted women. When Tag body spray was launched using the same position as Axe, consumers who had seen a Tag commercial reported that the brand advertised was Axe and Axe's share was unaffected by Tag's advertising.

Summary of Evaluating Creative

ADPLAN

The ADPLAN framework provides a conceptual tool for brand managers to assess advertising prior to engaging in empirical testing. By assessing attention distinctiveness, positioning, linkage, amplification and net equity, brand strategists can identify factors that might undermine the impact of advertising, and develop solutions to these problems prior to spending against a copy test.

The ADPLAN framework offers a structured approach to evaluating advertising copy. The effectiveness of advertising increases as advertising performs better on each of the ADPLAN criteria. Ads that are strong on attention and distinctiveness, but do not establish the brand's position invite consumers to develop their own view of the brand's position and allow competitors to usurp the brand's position. Thus, the goal in developing advertising is to ensure that the brand name is processed, and at the same time links the brand name to information about what goal the brand helps consumers achieve, and why it does so better than alternative brands. The Apple 1984 commercial exemplifies the achievement of these goals. It is arguably the most attention getting and distinctive commercial ever produced; but it not only got Apple noticed, it also presented the foundation of Apple's position by featuring a women engaged in unique actions. The female icon suggested communal, which provided the basis for Apple's user friendly benefit, and her unique actions distinguished the brand as being different from other platforms. These positioning elements were elaborated in subsequent campaigns and have been sustained over time.

Modifying the Creative on the Basis of the Ad Assessment

The advertiser (i.e., the client or brand manager) and the agency have distinct roles. The advertiser is in charge of developing the targeting and positioning strategy in conjunction with the ad agency and in evaluating how well the creative and media fit with the target and position established for the brand. The ad agency is responsible for developing the creative and media. If the advertiser's analysis using a device such as ADPLAN suggests that there are disparities between the strategy and its execution, it is the agency's responsibility to modify the advertising to resolve the disparities. In many cases, the advertiser attempts to facilitate this process by suggesting specific ways of fixing advertising ("make the logo bigger" "say zesty rather than tasty,"). This should be left to the agency. Most advertisers are not adept at developing copy or the artwork and their suggestions about how to perform these functions more often undermine advertising than facilitate it (for a humorous example go to the following link www.youtube.com/watch?v=xwqPYeTSYng).

Chapter Exercises

- Pick an execution and critique it using the ADPLAN framework. What strategic feedback would you give to the creative?

- Use ADPLAN to evaluate the Passat 2.0 ad.

- Find an example of an execution that uses late identification. Is the risk of late identification successfully attenuated? Why or why not?

Recommended Readings

Keller, Kevin Lane (1993), "Conceptualizing, Measuring, and Managing Customer-Based Brand Equity," *Journal of Marketing, 57* (January), 1–22.

Kent, Robert J. and Chris T. Allen (1994), "Competitive Interference Effects in Consumer Memory for Advertising: The Role of Brand Familiarity," *Journal of Marketing, 58* (July), 97-105.

Petty, Richard E. and John T. Cacioppo (1979), "Issue Involvement can Increase or Decrease Persuasion by Enhancing Message-relevant Cognitive Responses," *Journal of Personality and Social Psychology*, *37*, 1915-26.

Rucker, D. D. and Richard E. Petty (2006), "Increasing the Effectiveness of Communications to Consumers: Recommendations Based on the Elaboration Likelihood and Attitude Certainty Perspectives," *Journal of Public Policy and Marketing*, 25 (1), 39-52.

Empirically Measuring Advertising Effectiveness

Chapter 11

Chapter 11 Objectives

- Identify measures of advertising effectiveness
    - Measures of learning: Ad recall, brand recall, top-of-mind, perceptual measures and impressions.
    - Evaluative measures: Attitude, certainty, thoughts, moment-to-moment, physiological measures.
    - Behavioral measures: Purchase intention, brand switching, willingness to pay
- Evaluate the testing procedures typically used to measure ad effectiveness.
    - How many exposures to test ads should be used?
    - What aspects of the context in which testing is done are important to evaluate?

When Quaker Oats purchased Gatorade from Stokely Van Camp in 1983, Gatorade distribution was limited to the southern part of the US. Gatorade had been developed at the University of Florida ("the lemonade that Gators drank") and its distribution did not yet extend to the northern states. Thus, Southerners were likely to have been familiar with the brand, and even have tried it. In contrast, Northerners were likely to have had little familiarity with the brand, and in all likelihood they would not have consumed it. This circumstance raised the issue of whether a national advertising campaign was feasible, or whether two separate campaigns would be needed for each geographic area. Two campaigns were tested. One featured distinct advertising executions developed separately for southern and northern states on the assumption that different advertising would be needed to accommodate geographic differences in category and brand knowledge. The second campaign was a national spot that was intended to appeal to both segments by promoting the hydration needed for peak sports performance. Management had a strong preference for a single national campaign because the cost of creative and media was significantly lower for a national campaign than for two regional ones.

To determine whether it was feasible to run a national campaign, Quaker conducted a test market comprised of consumers from both regions to compare a campaign that would address Northerners' limited knowledge with one that was intended for all consumers regardless of their knowledge. The results of the test market suggested that both campaigns performed similarly in terms of liking and intention to buy Gatorade. The national campaign was then implemented due to its lower cost.

Testing advertising effectiveness can sometimes provide brand managers with a relatively low-cost means of evaluating the value of an ad campaign before making a substantial commitment to media. In this chapter, we examine approaches to measuring advertising effectiveness. This entails reviewing the measures that offer insight about ad effectiveness including indicators of learning, evaluation and behavior, and assessing the procedures used to determine ad effectiveness.

Measuring Advertising Effectiveness

Advertisers do have a choice in the selection of copy testing services, though these services have similar offerings. For TV advertising, most services recruit consumers to watch television programming in which the ads to be tested as well as control ads are inserted. Control ads are included to simulate the clutter conditions found in actual viewing situations. Prior to the viewing of these programs and ads, respondents are asked to indicate their brand preferences in several categories including the ones to be tested in order to establish a baseline. They are then shown the program and advertising material. When the presentation is complete, the audience is asked a series of questions based on the material that they have just viewed that pertain to what they learned and how they feel about the advertising and the advertised brand.

Copy tests have two purposes. One is to determine the impact of an ad. The other is to offer insight about why advertising had the effect observed. Though copy tests provide valuable information, testing results generally do not translate directly into real world outcomes. For example, a 10% increase in favorable attitude found in test does not necessarily mean that this same increase will be found when the advertising campaign is presented. Rather than being used as direct predictors for a brand's success in the marketplace, the test scores are used to compare different executions at a point in time, to evaluate a current creative in relation to its predecessors, or as variables in a model that attempts to predict sales. In addition, the copy testing services provide norms to be used as benchmarks in evaluating the effectiveness of all the ads being tested. As a starting point, we examine the value of frequently used ad effectiveness measures. Then we evaluate the procedures used to test advertising effectiveness.

Learning Measures

A series of measures are useful in assessing ad learning. Top-of-mind awareness and perceptual measures provide indicators that the brand name has been registered in memory, and measures of ad recall and brand recall offer an indication of what consumers have learned about a brand.

Top-of-Mind (TOM) Awareness. This involves using a category cue to prompt the retrieval of brand names that would be considered when purchasing the category. For example, top-of-mind brand recall might entail asking consumers to list the brands of beer they would consider when next purchasing beer. We refer to this measure of the consideration set TOM awareness. An increase in this type of awareness, as indicated by an increased presence of the advertised brand in the consideration set, is a valuable indicator of purchase likelihood. Developing a media schedule with greater repetition than that currently being used can combat low TOM awareness.

Perceptual Measures. In some situations, consumer learning of brand names is such that they cannot retrieve it from memory, but they do recognize it when they see the brand name. Billboards, signage at sporting events and on vehicles are often used to enhance brand name recognition. In these cases, perceptual measures might be useful. These measures tap whether advertising enhances the consumers' ability to recognize the brand name. This involves presenting consumers with information assessing the prominence of a brand name or other information. Along these lines, if the goal were to test the familiarity with the brand Bulls-eye after viewing advertising for it, a perceptual measure such as fragment completion would be appropriate. If respondents complete the fragment B--ls--- with "Bullseye" after seeing an ad for this brand, there would be evidence of perceptual learning, and of having paid attention to the ad.

Ad Recall. A majority of measures are based on the assumption that if consumers learn the content of an advertising message, this knowledge will enhance the likelihood that they will purchase the brand. Thus, in copy tests, consumers are asked to indicate the ads that they remember seeing. For the ads they remember, they are asked to describe what they have seen and what they have heard that was presented in the ad. If the respondents fail to recall the target ad, they are prompted with the target ad's category (e.g., "Do you remember seeing an ad for automobiles?"). If this fails to elicit memory of the target ad, they are given a brand prompt ("Do you remember an ad for VW?"). The recall data are typically available in the form of the respondents' verbatim responses as well as a summary score that reflects the percentage of viewers who demonstrated recall of critical message information. One measure often used to assess the advertising effectiveness of a specific ad is consumers' ability to provide verbatim recall of the advertising message content.

Although recall of the advertising content is a useful indicator of the extent to which consumers paid attention to the ad and what they learned from it, predicting the effectiveness of advertising in terms of how it affects consumer behavior in the marketplace on the basis of ad recall can lead to inaccurate conclusions. One problem in using measures that ask for some type of ad recall as an indicator of what information consumers attended to when exposed to an ad is that consumers often have difficulty tracing the origin of their knowledge once it has been represented in memory. This is because advertising information is associated with consumers' prior knowledge as part of the storage process. When asked to recall the contents of a specific ad, people can certainly conjure up brand-related information. The difficultly lies in determining whether the information they retrieve is based on the particular message that they are being asked about, some other message they might have seen for the brand, or self-generated knowledge. When the consumer experiences difficulty placing the origin of the information, this uncertainty causes them to underreport the information that they paid attention to and remember.

Consider consumers exposed to an advertisement for Tide detergent that introduces a new ingredient for getting out dirt. When asked to recall this information, consumers neglect to report the new ingredient that was described in the ad because they are not certain about whether they learned it from the ad or knew it from some other source. Conversely, in some cases consumers can accurately report ad information that they did not attend to during the ad in question. Campbell's soup ads typically describe the heartiness of the brand because of the quality ingredients. Consumers reporting this information in the copy test are deemed to have paid attention to the specific advertising in question, even if they relied on prior knowledge from past advertising rather than information from the ad they just viewed as a basis for their responses. Due to this tendency of consumers to both over report in situations where ad messaging is familiar and underreport at times when specific details are asked to be recalled, it is difficult to rely on ad recall as a true measure of ad learning.

Brand Recall. Consumers make purchase decisions based on what they know about a brand, rather than on what they remember from an ad. Thus, consumers' recall of information about a brand is an important indicator of ad effectiveness. Brand recall differs from ad recall in that it often solicits what people know without making reference to the origins of their knowledge. To determine what advertising contributed to this brand knowledge, an experiment is required where consumers are randomly assigned to alternative creative executions for the same brand. Thus, the differences in brand recall are a reflection of the attention paid to each ad and what was learned from each. When recall is low, greater media reach and amplification of the brand's benefits are warranted.

Although brand recall is indicative of what consumers know about a brand, it is often not an accurate predictor of consumers' behavior. This is because brand evaluations and choice are often not determined only by brand knowledge, but by consumers' idiosyncratic associations to that information (i.e., the amplification of the message). For example, consumers might exhibit good recall of an advertising claim that a shampoo is cheaper than the ones offered by the competition, but the response to this information could vary greatly. For some consumers, cheaper implies the product is of low quality, which limits their interest in purchasing the brand. For other consumers, the lower price could represent good value, and thus result in a greater inclination to purchase. Though in both cases the recall was accurate, these idiosyncratic responses to ad information make it difficult to predict purchase on the basis of recall alone. Evaluative measures offer additional insight by providing an indication about how people feel about their brand knowledge.

Evaluative Measures

Consumers' evaluations of a brand can be assessed by a variety of measures. These include attitudes, certainty, thoughts, moment-to-moment responses, and physiological responses. We describe and evaluate each of these measures.

Attitudes. Perhaps the most frequently used measure of dispositions is attitude. Attitude questions probe how consumers feel about a brand rather than what they know about it. An attitude represents a general evaluation of something, a degree of liking or disliking. Thus, message recipients are asked to evaluate a brand on general affective items such as like-dislike, good-bad and superior-inferior (see figure 11.1 for examples). In addition, sometimes more specific brand characteristics such as consumers' feelings about a brand's price and quality can be included. The more favorable consumers' attitudes toward the brand are after seeing advertising, the more effective is the ad.

Measurement of Consumer Attitudes:

Please circle the number that best reflects your opinion about eating at FuddRuckers

Good	1	2	3	4	5	6	7	Bad
Pleasant	1	2	3	4	5	6	7	Unpleasant
Like	1	2	3	4	5	6	7	Dislike

Measurement of Consumer Attitude Certainty:

How certain are you of your opinion towards FuddRuckers?

Uncertain	1	2	3	4	5	6	7	Certain

How convinced are you that your opinion towards FuddRuckers is Correct?

Unconvinced	1	2	3	4	5	6	7	Convinced

Measurement of Consumer Thoughts:

Write down all the thoughts you have about FuddRuckers.

Figure 11.1: Sample Evaluative Measures

Certainty. A problem encountered in using attitude measures, particularly for an established brand, is that this measure lacks sensitivity. Attitudes represent lasting general impressions and unless advertising is delivering significant brand news, attitudes toward a brand are often likely to be unaffected by advertising in the short run.

Consider an ad for Kraft cheese that describes its nutritional value. This ad is not likely to change consumers' attitudes toward the brand because they are likely to have learned this information from prior Kraft advertising. However, this does not necessarily imply that consumers' are unaffected by Kraft advertising.

Even when attitudes are not affected, consumers' certainty about their attitude might be influenced by the presentation of advertising. Research by Derek Rucker and colleagues demonstrates that a joint calculation of how favorable consumers are towards a product (i.e., their attitude) and how certain they are of their attitude (i.e., attitude certainty) offers a more accurate means of predicting consumers' behavioral tendencies than the use of attitudes alone. The finding is that when advertising enhances certainty in a favorable attitude, there is an increase in the likelihood that consumers will engage in the behavior advocated in the ad, even when the attitude toward the brand is not affected by the advertising.

Thoughts. Another attitude measure involves the solicitation of consumers' thoughts in response to an advertisement. Thoughts often underlie consumers' attitudes and thus can be used to diagnose why an execution created a favorable or unfavorable attitudinal response. For example, an individual might hold a negative attitude towards a fast food restaurant because when thinking about it they conjure up the thought that the fries are dripping in oil. Such thoughts would be valuable in guiding modifications to the advertising. In contrast, consumers' thoughts about how to fix advertising are typically not helpful.

Moment-to-moment measures. Measures have been devised to evaluate consumers' moment-to-moment interest in what is being presented in an ad. One such measure entails having respondents turn a dial to indicate the level of their moment-to-moment interest of an advertisement. Often, interpretation proceeds in a literal way where those portions of an ad that yield high interest are considered effective, whereas portions corresponding to weak interest are deemed ineffective. Advertisers frequently use these results to omit low interest portions of the ads or to elaborate further on those portions of the ad deemed more interesting. As intuitive as this approach is, there is evidence that other ways to assess moment-to-moment responses are more diagnostic in predicting ad effectiveness. The general trend in interest over the commercial and the level of peak interest might be more indicative of ad effectiveness than is the response to a specific portion of the copy. Even if these indicators are used, moment-to-moment measures require an active response such as turning a dial that could draw attention away from the content of the ad itself and potentially influence the evaluation of the ad and responses to other measures. Baumgartner, Sujan, and Padgett (1997) offer a detailed discussion of moment-to-moment measures.

Physiological Measures. Some copy tests attempt to bolster traditional evaluative measures with indicators of consumers' physiological responses during ad exposure. Pupil dilation, eye movement and voice stress, among other measures, have been used for this purpose. These measures might be perceived as attractive because interpretation of an ad's impact is uncontaminated by the researcher's questions, the sample, and misinterpretations of respondent answers. However, these measures should be used with caution. Pupil dilation measures are responsive to both changes in attention and changes in luminosity. When an ad confounds these factors, unequivocal interpretation of changes in dilation is not possible.

Another test tracks eye movement to determine the pattern consumers' eyes follow as they move across a page as well as in what spots they hold their gaze. This type of testing can be used in the evaluation of what consumers' find interesting as well as what they are and are not seeing in the ad.

Voice stress has also been used for a number of years to assess ad effectiveness, but correlates of this measure have been difficult to find, thus making its interpretation an elusive task (see Horvath 1982). In a voice stress analysis, a vocal response is measured for a wide range of emotions, including excitement, confusion and attention and is digitally analyzed. Voice stress seems to be used most frequently to test advertising for brands in decline. Perhaps this is because managers realize that the probability of turning the brand around with a new campaign is low and they wish to deflect responsibility to a presumably objective measure rather than to themselves.

An emerging technology involves the use of functional magnetic resonance imaging (fMRI) and more conventional electroencephalograms (EEGs) to observe which areas of the brain light up when test subjects view or hear various promotions. To date, it has been shown that different regions of the cortex are responsive to different stimuli, but the unique contribution of these measures to an assessment of ad effectiveness is still to be determined.

Behavioral Measures

Behavioral measures offer insight about the effectiveness of advertising. This might involve conducting a test market where different ads or different levels of exposures are presented in different but comparable markets, and consumers' purchase is tracked over time. Alternatively, a service such as Behaviorscan can be used. This service utilizes a split cable within a particular market so that different strategies can be tested on people living in the same block. The cable allows the advertiser to vary the ad content that is shown to different consumers, the number of exposures to advertising that they receive, and other communication variables. When consumers purchase at supermarkets, drug and other outlets, they swipe a card that indicates what was purchased, the quantity bought and whether or not it was on sale. Thus, the advertiser is informed about the ads to which the consumer was exposed and the purchases made in the advertised category after ad exposure. In this way the effect of different advertising strategies on consumer purchase can be determined.

While measures of actual behavior offer important information about the effect of advertising, their cost often prompts the use of proxies for behavior. Measures such as purchase intention, willingness to pay and brand switching/loyalty fall into this category.

Purchase Intention and Willingness to Pay. One type of behavior measure is whether consumers anticipate buying a product after seeing an ad for it. This is information is usually acquired by asking consumers their intentions after viewing and ad for the brand and comparing the responses to those who have not been exposed to the advertising. An alternative indicator of purchase likelihood is willingness to pay which is tested by asking the consumer to provide an average amount they would be willing to pay for a product. Again the impact of advertising is compared to a control group that was not exposed to the advertising. The assumption is that to the extent an advertisement increases consumers' perception of brand value, it has the potential to increase their likelihood of buying the brand.

Brand Switching and Loyalty. Copy tests often include measures of choice. The brand switching potential of an ad is assessed by the change in brand preference as a result of ad exposure. Consumers are asked to record various brand preferences prior to viewing the ad presentation and then repeat this process after viewing the advertising. This measure is of interest when the goal of advertising is to promote brand switching. In many cases, however, the goal is to sustain current user loyalty. When this is the case, the use of choice as a measure of ad effectiveness requires the assumption that the same execution that best promotes switching also best sustains loyalty. At a minimum, it would be useful to develop a procedure that tests this assumption. Alternatively, when the goal is to maintain brand loyalty, it might be useful to examine how advertising enhances consumers' repeat purchase behavior in the category. Because accumulating responses on this measure is costly and time consuming, a proxy for loyalty can be used. This proxy involves evaluating whether brand loyalty is sustained when a target ad is presented in the context of other ads in the same category. Along these lines, an experiment can be done in which the target ad is presented in the context of ads for competitive brands or in the context of ads for brands in other categories. The extent to which consumers sustain their purchase of the target brand in the competitive and noncompetitive contexts offers a measure of loyalty: the smaller the difference in loyalty between these contexts, the greater is the loyalty.

What Measure Do You Use?

What measure should be used to assess the effectiveness of an ad? The measures we have discussed provide the greatest insight when used in concert. Behaviors in response to advertising are informative about the outcome of exposures to advertising. Learning and evaluation measures provide diagnostics that are informative about why advertising had the effect it did. A lack of brand learning in a copy test indicates that the advertising does not provide the motivation needed to process ad information. Good ad performance on learning measures, but unfavorable brand evaluation implies that the position and creative require modification. And the presence of both learning and favorable evaluation suggest that the advertising will have impact on behavior providing that other elements of the marketing mix facilitate this outcome.

Testing Procedures

When testing ads, it is important not only to consider measures that are to be administered, but also the procedures used to elicit consumers' responses. We consider issues with regard to the number of exposures to advertising used to test ad effectiveness and the context that surrounds the advertisement being tested.

Number of Exposures

Copy testing procedures usually entail showing the target ad once or several times within the context of programming material as well as other ads from different product categories than the target ad. The assumption is that if execution A is superior to execution B (or a benchmark based on past test results) at the test level of ad exposures, this relationship will be preserved regardless of the actual level of exposures when the advertising is aired or printed. Thus, if three exposures to a Tylenol ad in which brand claims are made about headache relief outperforms three exposures to a Tylenol ad where the brand is shown relieving muscle aches, the assumption is that this superiority would persist whether these ads were tested at one or 10 exposures. This assumption is likely to hold when the alternative executions being tested are similar in the processing demands they impose. However, when one ad requires more effort than another to process, inferences from copy tests might be inaccurate.

To illustrate this issue, consider the impact of three different executions for the same brand of ice cream. In this illustration, the effort required for people to comprehend the message content is varied by how the message is presented. In Ad 1, a message about the brand is sung to music. This ad is the most effortful to process as the message recipient must listen to the music and decipher the lyrics at the same time. In Ad 2, moderate effort is required as the recipients are told the main message theme which is then followed by the same theme being sung to music. Finally, Ad 3 requires the least processing and entails the message being read dramatically.

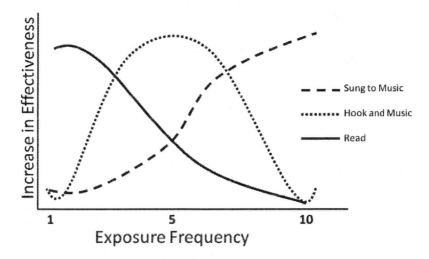

Figure 11.2: Effectiveness as a Function of Execution and Exposures

As illustrated in figure 11.2, the ad that requires the most processing also requires repeated exposures to be fully effective. Increasing exposures to this ad increases the likelihood that people will comprehend what is communicated about the brand and thus enhance their favorableness toward it. For Ad 2, people first learn the message content, which make them favorable to the product, and then activate their own thoughts, which are less favorable than the information presented in the ad, which is developed with the explicit purpose of being persuasive. Thus, there is a decline in ad effectiveness as exposures mount. A different outcome emerges for the least effortful ad to process, Ad 3, which is the one that is read dramatically. Here, the simplicity of the ad allows people to learn its contents with a single exposure. Additional message repetition results in wearout and prompts people to activate their own thoughts about the product, which results in a decline in message persuasion. These outcomes indicate that the read message would be most effective at one exposure, the hook with music most effective at five exposures, and the ad that is sung to music most effective at ten exposures. Thus, which ad to use would depend on the planned average frequency of the target consumer. A more detailed description of the effects described here is provided by Anand and Sternthal (1990).

Importance of Context

In developing procedures to measure advertising effectiveness, it is important to consider the context in which the target ad will be presented. Most copy testing services employ a context composed of television programming and ads for products that have membership in product categories unrelated to the target ad. There is evidence that this context might be biased in favor of ads that feature a brand's image rather than brand attributes.

To clarify why this might occur, consider two ads for a camera. The attribute-focused ad enumerates brand attributes about the flash and shutter speeds and shows pictures of these features. The other ad is image-focused. It enumerates the same attributes as the first ad, but in lieu of pictures of product features, it shows vacation pictures taken by the camera. The image ad is likely to be more persuasive than the attribute ad when shown in a context of unrelated ads. This is because the image ad prompts a recall of the fact that there was an ad for a camera by relating it to vacations, and the unrelated context makes it easy to recall the features of the target because it was the only brand in the category presented. In contrast, the attribute-focused ad is more persuasive in a competing context of other camera ads because it facilitates the recall of the specific features of the target camera, a task made difficult by the presentation of the target brand in the context of other camera ads. Thus, the correspondence between test and real-world context is an important consideration in developing the testing environment. A more detailed discussion of context ad interactions is presented by Malaviya, Kisielius and Sternthal (1996).

Maximizing the Effectiveness of Copy Tests

Advertisers are interested in what consumers know about their brand and how favorable this knowledge is for two reasons. One is to assess the effectiveness of an ad. The other is to identify why an ad had the effect it did, which can be used to guide the modification of an ad. Several considerations are appropriate in developing measures of advertising effectiveness:

1. Consumers' behavior in response to advertising is an important measure because it informs marketers about the effect of advertising. However, such a response does not provide guidance about how to enhance ad effectiveness when this goal is relevant. Learning and attitude measures are of interest because they provide insight about why consumers exhibited the behavior that they did and thus offer a starting point for how to make advertising more effective.

2. Procedures are needed to estimate the exposure elasticity of advertising effectiveness. At issue is whether increasing exposures to advertising will enhance or diminish the impact of advertising. This knowledge will offer insight about whether the superiority of one execution over another in copy testing is likely to be sustained when different levels of ad exposure are employed in everyday settings.

3. The context in which target advertising is evaluated might bias the outcomes in terms of a particular type of execution. This observation questions the adequacy of procedures in which advertising is assessed in the absence of programming and other ads. This implies that it is important to select advertising testing contexts that correspond to the milieu in which advertising will appear. This includes both the media vehicle (e.g., the television show, website, or magazine) as well as the other advertisements featured in that media. If the context is composed only of ads for brands in categories other than the target ad, an assessment of brand linkage is problematic.

Summary of Empirically Measuring Advertising Effectiveness

The testing of advertising effectiveness serves an important control function. Tests can be informative of the demand that will be generated by a campaign. Equally important, tests of advertising effectiveness provide a diagnostic that indicates why advertising has had the effect observed and thus provides a basis for enhancing the impact of an ad. Performing tests of advertising effectiveness allow the advertiser to make an assessment of the advertising investment before committing resources to media, which represent the bulk of the ad expenditure. Furthermore, as a manager acquires test data over time, they can provide benchmarks to guide future campaign evaluations.

Chapter Exercises

- You are a brand manager for M&M and Mars. You are in charge of promoting both an original candy bar (e.g., Snickers) and a new flavor (e.g., Strawberry Snickers). Creative has given you a new print execution for each brand as well as banner ads to be placed on the internet. What metrics would you want to assess your test? Does the desirability of the metrics change as a function of assessing the advertising for the original candy bar versus the new flavor?

- In a previous campaign you found that four exposures of a television spot led to the most effectiveness in changing consumers' evaluations and purchasing intentions. Under what circumstances would this benchmark of four exposures likely be an appropriate one for testing against future executions? Under what circumstances would you be more likely to need to develop a new benchmark or vary exposure rates in your test? Are there circumstances were the media dictate the number of exposures?

Recommended Readings

Anand, Punam and Brian Sternthal (1993). "The Effects of Program Involvement and Ease of Message Counterarguing on Advertising Persuasiveness," *Journal of Consumer Psychology,* 1, 225-238.

Baumgartner, Hans, Mita Sujan, and Dan Padgett (1997), "Patterns of Affective Reactions to Ads: Integration of Moment-by-Moment Reactions Into Overall Judgments,"*Journal of Marketing Research,* 34, 219-232.

Horvath, Frank (1982), "Detecting Deception: The Problem and Reality of Voice Stress Analysis," *Journal of Forensic Sciences, 27,* 340-351.

Malaviya, Prashant, Jolita Kisielius, and Brian Sternthal (1996), "The Effect of Type of Elaboration on Ad Processing and Judgment," *Journal of Marketing Research,* 33, 410-421.

Rucker, Derek D., and Richard E. Petty (2006)," Increasing Effectiveness of Communications to Consumers: Recommendations Based on the Elaboration Likelihood and Attitude Certainty Perspectives," *Journal of Public Policy and Marketing, 25* (1), 39-52.

Rucker, Derek D., Richard E. Petty, and Joseph R. Priester (2007), "Understanding Advertising Effectiveness from a Psychological Perspective: The Importance of Attitudes and Attitude Strength," In Gerald. J. Tellis & T. Ambler (Eds.), *The Handbook of Advertising* (pp. 71-88), Thousand Oaks, CA: Sage.

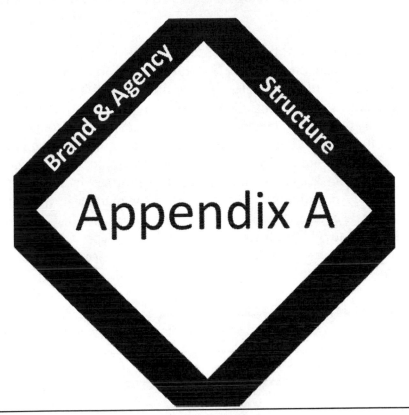

Appendix A

Appendix A Objectives

- Provide an understanding of the structure of brands and advertising agencies
- Understand client-agency interactions

Today's advertisers are faced with the challenge of developing effective advertising in a financially driven environment. The search for advertising efficiencies has prompted efforts to globalize advertising strategy. At the same time, greater ad effectiveness is sought by developing better consumer insight as a basis for advertising strategy. Advertisers have also attempted to improve the impact of their ad expenditure by changing how they employ various agency resources in making planning, media, marketing services and internet decisions. And, advertisers have changed the manner in which they compensate agencies for their services. Agencies have had to reinvent themselves to address their clients' needs. This appendix describes the advertiser-agency relationship in the context of these developments.

Rank	Parent Company	Ad Dollars Spent (USD, in million)
1	Procter & Gamble Co.	$4,189
2	Verizon Communications	$3,020
3	AT&T	$2,797
4	General Motors Co.	$2,214
5	Pfizer	$2,097
6	Johnson & Johnson	$2,060
7	Walt Disney Co.	$2,003
8	Time Warner	$1,848
9	L'Oreal	$1,833
10	Kraft Foods	$1,748

Table A.1: Leading Advertisers,
Source: Nielsen, December 15th, 2008, http://www.nielsen.com

Advertisers

At the end of 2008, total measured media spending in the U.S. is estimated to be $258.7 billion, which represents a 7.6% decline from the preceding year. Major advertisers include automobile manufacturers, pharmaceutical firms, communication and technology marketers, and food and beverage companies. In addition to this media spending, there is about another $100 billion in unmeasured media, which includes sales promotion, co-op spending, coupons, catalogs, business and farm publications and special events. A detailed analysis of ad spending trends is found in *Advertising Age's* "100 Leading National Advertisers report" (http://www.adage.com). The largest US advertisers are shown in table A.1.

Consumer products companies and other firms that advertise extensively generally employ a brand organization system to perform the advertising function. This type of organization is depicted in figure A.1.

Figure A.1: Brand Organization

Line management involves an assistant brand manager whose chief responsibility is to ensure that the brand manager has the data needed to make marketing decisions and to support the execution of the marketing strategy. Brand managers are involved in strategy development and are responsible for coordinating with manufacturing, finance, research and other support functions. They also have primary responsibility for the execution of marketing strategy. Category managers are responsible for the development of strategy and the management of the relations within the distribution channel.

In dealing with an ad agency, the client's task is to develop the advertising strategy, which includes segmentation, targeting and positioning. The client also assesses the extent to which the execution developed by the agency corresponds with the strategy and to request that the agency address any lack of correspondence. It is not the client's responsibility to fix off-strategy executions. Most clients are not capable of copy writing and art direction. These tasks are best left to the agency.

While the organizational structure in figure A.1 represents the approach followed by many firms, innovations are emerging. Procter & Gamble introduced Market Development Organizations (MDOs) to complement their brand management structure. Whereas traditional line management such as that depicted in figure A.1 has responsibility for product, packaging and advertising, MDOs serve another function. Their responsibility is to work as sales teams to develop co-marketing programs with retailers, reconfigure the placement and merchandising of products within the store, develop relationships with other marketers, and design new approaches to reach attractive segments such as the Hispanic and African American markets. In effect, the store is viewed as a marketing medium. Retailers benefit from sophisticated merchandising of their offerings and the MDOs benefit from the detailed consumer information collected by retailers as part of conducting business.

In the past several years, there have also been a substantial number of changes in advertisers' needs and goals. To an increasing extent, advertisers are faced with the dilemma of having to promote parity products with a limited advertising budget on a global basis. This challenge has increased advertisers need for greater consumer insight so that effective marketing and advertising programs might be designed even in the absence of product differentiation and substantial ad budgets. With the downsizing that was common in the past decade, internal resources to provide this information were often lacking. Advertisers thus have turned to consulting firms, advertising agencies, and other outside firms to facilitate their advertising planning.

Efforts to market parity products effectively also has prompted a greater focus on neglected segments, particularly Hispanic and African American consumers, who collectively represent about one quarter of the American population. In addition, the emerging opportunities for segmentation and the pressure to limit ad spending have increased advertisers' interest in alternative media such as events, direct marketing and public relations. Approaches to developing integrated marketing communications (IMC), which involve selecting and coordinating various media vehicles, have become a topic of substantial interest. The role of the Internet in the corporate communication arsenal has emerged as a key issue in developing integrated marketing communications.

Finally, there is a growing determination to develop global advertising strategies. Although the executional elements of advertising vary from country to country, more and more firms are attempting to develop a global brand position. For example, P&G, which had a global strategy only for Pantene, Always, and Pringles a decade ago, now has many of its brands following a global strategy.

Agencies

Advertising agencies are organized in a manner similar to their clients, as the following descriptions and agency organization chart indicate (figure A.2).

Plans Board: Reviews the advertising developed for each client. This includes examining the objectives and budget, as well as the creative and media strategy.

Executive Committee: Seeks new business and organizes presentations to attract new clients.

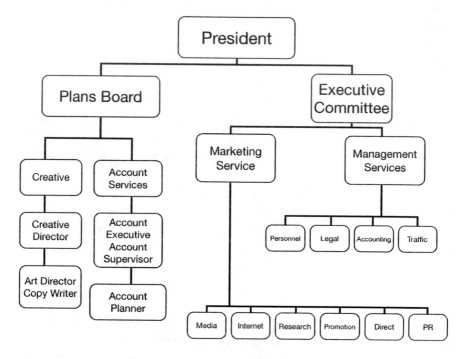

Figure A.2: Agency Organization

Creative: Creative includes copywriters who develop the copy for advertising and art directors who develop the layout and artwork for the advertising copy. They report to a creative director, who has a background in copywriting or art direction.

Account Services: The account services group includes account supervisors and account executives (AEs), who are responsible for the management of the client's advertising. This entails coordinating activities of the creative, media and research departments and serving as the agency's liaison to the client.

Account Planning: Planners are responsible for developing consumer insight so that advertising reliably reflects the voice of the consumer. Planners also conduct research designed to guide and enhance preliminary creative work. Planners generally have the same status as AEs within the agency, but are presented as AEs' subordinates to the client. This distances the planner from the client and allows the planner to have perspective.

Marketing Services: Conduct or contract research. Marketing services may include a department specializing in public relations, direct marketing and consumer promotions.

Media Services: Media planners develop the media plan, media objectives, and the selection of media vehicles. Media buyers negotiate the purchase of space and time.

Internet: Develops databases, web pages and Internet advertising for clients. This function also involves the development of a communication strategy for clients. Measurement of ad performance in terms of exposure to advertising, click throughs, and purchase is often performed as part of the Internet activity.

Management Services: This group includes a personnel department responsible for hiring and fostering the development of personnel, a legal department that reviews the fairness of advertising prior to its media dissemination, and accounting, which supervises payroll and payment to the media. Traffic is responsible for ensuring that client advertising done by the agency is made available in a timely manner to the appropriate mass media for airing or printing.

Full service ad agencies generally have the organizational structure and perform the tasks outlined above. However, there have been dramatic changes during the past few years in how ad agencies do business. As noted earlier, many agencies now have account planners who are charged with developing consumer insight for their clients. Media departments in many agencies are now divisions that have separate profit and loss responsibility. Along these lines, Publicis' media agency is Starcom MediaVest Group and Omnicom's media agency is OMD Worldwide. Because of their substantial media purchases, these departments offer the advertiser better efficiencies in media buying. As a result, an agency's media services group often competes for accounts from clients who have their creative done at some other ad agency. Marketing services departments and Internet expertise provide clients with media alternatives to supplement traditional broadcast and print media.

Agencies have also developed other capabilities to keep abreast of their clients' needs. Advertising to Hispanics and African Americans, which was once handled by agencies specializing in these minority segments, is now handled within general market agencies. This has been achieved largely through the acquisition of minority-oriented agencies by major ad agencies. For example, Burrell Communications, which was the largest agency in the African-American segment with $173.9 million in billings, was acquired by Publicis.

Rank	Agency	Revenue (USD)
1	WPP	$13,598 Billion
2	Omnicom Group	$11,721 Billion
3	Publicis Groupe	$6,287 Billion
4	Interpublic Group of Cos.	$6,028 Billion
5	Dentsu	$3,113 Billion
6	Aegis Group	$2,109 Billion
7	Havas	$2,010 Billion
8	Hakuhodo DY Holdings	$1,522 Billion
9	Acxiom Corp.	$750 Million
10	MDC Partners	$546 Million

Table A.2: Top Ten AD Organizations based on 2008 Revenue, Source: Advertising Age

Although there is a trend among advertisers to allocate the various advertising tasks to different firms on a piece-meal basis, there is also a trend toward consolidating the advertising function among a small number of agencies. Large agencies have been in an acquisition mode to satisfy their clients' need for a global presence, to provide direct marketing, PR and other marketing services that are the basis for integrated marketing communications, and to offer clients' superior media selection and buying efficiencies. The result of this strategy is the presence of ad organizations composed of several ad agencies. The largest ten ad organizations, by 2008 revenue, are shown in table A.2.

Within the ad organizations, there are ad agency brands. The top 10 agency brands in terms of worldwide revenue are shown in table A.3. The high variance in growth during the past year reflects the volatility in ad spending for advertisers in different product categories and the movement of accounts from one agency to another.

Rank	Agency Brand	Revenue (USD)	% Change
1	Dentsu	$2.3 Billion	-5.6%
2	McCann Erickson Worldwide	$1.4 Billion	15.0%
3	BBDO Worldwide	$1.1 Billion	-17.2%
4	DDB Worldwide	$1.1 Billion	-9.4%
5	JWT	$1.1 Billion	-11.8%
6	TBWA Worldwide	$1.0 Billion	-10.3%
7	Hakuhodo	$956 Million	-10.1%
8	Y&R	$931 Million	-10.1%
9	Publicis	$892 Million	-16.7%
10	Leo Burnett Worldwide	$777 Million	-6.2%

Table A.3: Top Ten Agency Brands Worldwide based on 2009 Revenue, Source: Advertising Age

Agency Selection

Advertisers can make or buy the advertising function. The decision to perform the advertising function in-house is typically made for several reasons. It is attractive when the cost of performing the function is lower than the amount received in media commission. In-house agencies are also attractive when there is a need for quick decision-making, or when the creative has the potential of being controversial. In this latter case, agencies are often reluctant to participate for fear of alienating their other clients. The decision to do advertising in-house assumes that the firm has the marketing acumen to develop and execute the advertising strategy and that the presence of a second opinion on the business will not be missed or will be compensated for in some other manner.

Once the decision to use an agency is made, several criteria are generally used to select the specific firm. One important criterion is expertise with the category or brand. Agencies that are familiar with the client's business are preferred to ones that are less familiar with it. Typically this expertise emerges because an agency has had a previous client in the industry of interest. For example, in the airline industry it is not uncommon for carriers to select an agency that has been recently fired by another airline. It is sometimes judicious, however, to select an agency with no category experience. When this is done, it is often with the goal of prompting the agency to develop fresh insights about consumers and to increase the chances that the creative execution does not closely resemble that of competitors.

Agency style is another important factor in agency selection. Agencies acquire a reputation for a particular style and advertisers select agencies whose approach corresponds with their perceived needs. Leo Burnett is known for the development of a big idea as exemplified in their campaigns for Green Giant. Hal Riney is recognized for his intuitive approach to advertising new products including Perrier and Saturn. Fallon is generally viewed as being on the cutting edge of creativity as exemplified by their campaign for Lee jeans, EDS, and ex-client Miller Lite (Dick). Wieden & Kennedy is recognized for its attitude campaigns for clients such as Nike. Goodby, Silverstein & Partners has a reputation for using consumer insight to do breakthrough advertising as evidenced in their Got Milk campaign and their Bud lizards spots. Crispen, Porter, & Bogusky is associated with edgy advertising as exemplified in their creative work for Burger King, and for its use of non-traditional advertising vehicles as illustrated by its advertising for Mini Cooper (e.g., purchasing seats at a nationally televised baseball game and placing a Mini in the seats).

Size has become an increasingly important criterion in selecting an agency. Large advertisers frequently desire agencies that are sufficiently large to have a local presence or to have the ability to mount a local presence on a global basis. Advertisers are also increasingly attracted to agencies that have the sophistication to handle the complexity of today's media strategy development and buying, though it is increasingly the case that media and creative functions are delivered piece-meal by different agencies. When advertisers have cutting edge creative needs, smaller agencies are often considered for the creative task. Clients' need for the services that are best delivered by both large and small agencies, has given ad organizations an advantage because these organizations include both types of firms.

Relations between the personnel of the agency and its client are important determinants of agency selection and particularly of agency longevity with a client. Over time, the relations between top management of the agency and client often deepen and this helps sustain agency longevity. More often than not, an agency is terminated when the relations between the senior management of the agency and client sour, or when the personal relationship is lost because of new management on either the client or agency side. Leo Burnett, for example, lost the $120 million United Airlines account after a 31-year relationship when senior management at United and Burnett retired at the same time.

During the past several years, there has been a decline in the length of client-agency relations. An unusually high number of long-lived relationships between advertiser and agency have been terminated. Beyond the United account, Burnett lost the McDonald's business, which it had held since the early 1980s, J. Walter Thompson lost the Kodak business that it had acquired in 1930, N.W. Ayer was fired by AT&T after an 88 year relationship and Foote, Cone, and Belding lost long-time client Gatorade when Pepsi acquired Quaker Oats. A recent survey reported that, on average, client-agency relations now last between five and six years.

Agency Compensation

In 1841, Volney Palmer established the first advertising agency in Boston. Palmer operated as a broker who brought advertiser and medium together, a service for which he charged the medium a commission of 25%. Palmer's legacy is the commission system that was the primary means of agency compensation for the next 150 years. It involves having the advertiser pay the agency for advertising space and time purchased. In turn, the agency pays the medium and the medium provides a commission, typically 15% of billings, to the agency. For example, when an advertiser buys $1 million of time from a television network, the advertiser pays the network this amount through the agency. The network pays the advertiser's agency a commission of $150,000.

In recent years, there has been a dramatic shift in the way agencies are compensated. In 1990, Y&R and Needham ad agencies began to advocate a performance-based compensation. Under this plan, the agency's compensation was a reflection of the client's success. During the next several years, few clients embraced this compensation alternative. In 1992, almost 60% of the agency compensation was in the form of commissions, and more than half of this was at the standard rate of 15%. The next several years saw a reduction in the percent of agency-client relations that were commission based, and of those who were, the percent paying 15% dropped to about 20%. By 1997, only 35% of the agency contracts were commission based. Over 50% were fee based and 30% of the contracts included incentive compensation agreements. This trend toward performance-based compensation has continued to grow during the past several years as major advertisers such as Sears, Colgate, Kraft, Procter & Gamble, McDonalds Ford and General Motors have embraced the concept. Currently, more than two-thirds of advertisers use some from of performance-based compensation.

An increasing number of clients are attracted to a performance-based system because it involves having the agency share the risk with the client. In some situations, the agency is compensated on the basis of sales and market share. While there are aspects of the marketing plan that the agency does not control, larger firms have begun to develop models that factor out marketing variables other than advertising and thus they are able to estimate the contribution of advertising. It is also common for advertisers' performance to be judged on the basis of communication criteria such as brand awareness and brand preference rather than sales response.

One of the ramifications of performance-based compensation is that it changes the way agencies approach the communication task. Several years ago, Anheuser-Busch developed a goal of increasing the number of Bud Light tap handles in pubs. Its agency, DDB Needham, was given this assignment, for which they were to be compensated in accord with the increase in Bud Light tap handles. Their strategy was to offer beer drinkers the opportunity to star in a local Bud Light commercial. To select a winner, casting calls were held at participating pubs, which added taps for the event. People mobbed the participating bars and consumed large quantities of beer while waiting to audition.

The squeeze in agency compensation has been going on for several decades. It has resulted in a significant reduction in the number of agency personnel. In the early '70s the rule of thumb was about 10 people for every million dollars in billings (i.e., total $ placed for a client in space and time--not agency revenue). By the mid-1980s, the average number of people for each million dollars in billings had fallen to about 2.4, and currently it is under one person per million in billings. Whereas agency CEOs were responsible for overseeing new business acquisition and monitoring the performance of current clients, in many agencies they now also work on client businesses.

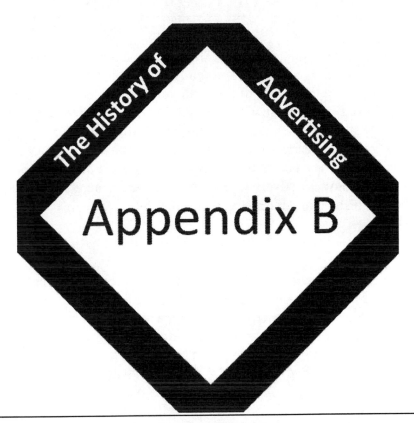

The History of Advertising

Appendix B

| **Appendix B Objectives** |

- Provide a brief history of advertising in the United States depicting major developments from the early 19th century
- Provide an understanding of advertising's past to understand its future

This appendix highlights the role of advertisers, advertising agencies, and media in developing advertising and serves as a basis for anticipating the nature of future developments in the institutions that guide advertising practice. The antecedents of current advertising practice can be understood by tracing the history of advertising during the past 150 years. Furthermore, understanding the history of advertising provides a basis for predicting the nature of contemporary changes in how the advertising function is performed. For convenience, the history of advertising is divided into seven eras.[*]

Pre-1900: Era of Evolution

The Industrial Revolution prompted increased interest in extending the sale of goods beyond local markets. At the same time, newspapers began to emerge as the primary means of mass communication in the United States. By the middle of the nineteenth century, there were over 1700 newspapers in the country.

Newspaper advertising during the first half of the 19th century was restricted in terms of the size and content of the ads. Advertising had to fit a half-inch square and could only include copy. In response to these constraints, advertisers of every day products began to experiment with so-called *iteration advertising*. This entailed repeating a slogan such as "Royal Baking Powder is Absolutely Pure" or "Use Sapolio" as many times as would fit in the space. Media scheduling often focused on placing ads in the same publications repeatedly so that the audience would receive multiple exposures of the advertising message. These slogans became the predominant approach to print advertising by the turn of the century and represent the antecedents for slogans such as Milk's "Got Milk" and Burger King's "Have it your way."

During the second half of the 19th century, a number of developments began to change the nature of advertising. The population of the country grew rapidly, spurred by liberal immigration policies.

[*] The contribution made by Melissa Waters to the historical analysis is acknowledged with thanks.

Between 1830 and 1860, the population of the United States grew from a little over 10 million people to over 30 million. The population also became more literate: Illiteracy fell to about 10% by 1900. The number of magazines grew from under 700 at the time of the Civil War to about 3300 in 1885. And transportation improved considerably as railways were built to link all parts of the country. Thus, by the turn of the century there was a substantial population throughout the country that could read and be reached by both mass media and the distribution system.

To attract national markets, manufacturers began to brand their goods following the Civil War. For example, Soup became Campbell's Soup. By the 1870s, brands such as Coca Cola, Maxwell House and Levis had been established. Magazines became the vehicles of choice to make consumers aware of branded products. Starting with Volney Palmer in the mid-1800s, advertising agencies emerged as brokers between the advertiser and the media. Agencies helped their clients choose particular magazines on the basis of the type of audience the publications attracted. Segmentation was implemented by choosing magazines that delivered women, farmers, religious believers, or sports fans. Advertisers also selected magazines on the basis of the number of readers they attracted. Magazine publishers enhanced the attractiveness of their vehicles by lowering the price consumers paid for their magazines. To ensure the profitability of their publications, they began to sell space to advertisers. The legacy of this practice is that today, advertisers rather than readers account for the majority of a publication's revenues.

The agency's function as a broker between advertiser and medium changed in the latter part of the 1800s. Agencies were caught between getting the best prices for their clients and currying favor with media who were the source of their revenues. They resolved this conflict by adopting an open-contract-plus-commission plan that allowed the advertiser to know what agencies paid for space. Agencies also sought to differentiate themselves by adding to the services that they offered their clients. Of these, creative and art services were the most important. Ads made around the turn of the century often included entertainers and sports figures as product endorsers, the forerunner of today's spokespeople. Finally, agencies began to oversee the quality control of media choices. Clients' demands that media choices be justified led to the creation of Audit Bureau of Circulation (ABC), a service that provides certified readership for advertising vehicles.

1900-1929: Era of Creative Development

During the early 1900s, work by psychologists such as Walter Dill Scott (who was also president of Northwestern University) and Daniel Starch influenced how advertising messages were developed. Their notion was that advertising should make it easy to learn the brand name and the brand benefit. This was achieved by the use of mnemonic devices in advertising copy. Slogans and images, such as Ivory's "99 44/100 per cent pure," Prudential's "Rock of Gibraltar," and Schlitz's "the beer that made Milwaukee famous," emerged in the early 20th century. Similar advertising is used today in contexts such as political advertising, where brand name recognition and a sound bite platform are important determinants of voter choice.

After World War I, advertisers began to recognize that women made the majority of the consumer products purchases. This prompted advertisers to focus their advertising on women. To resonate with the female head of household, slice-of-life advertising was used that depicted everyday situations in which the brand was presented as the hero. When radio was introduced to the mass market in 1921, broadcast stations were prohibited from advertising. By the following year, radio advertising in the form of program sponsorship was sanctioned. Advertising agencies applied their print practice of charging the media rather than the advertiser for their services to radio. Agencies were often instrumental in developing radio programming, which was sold to sponsors. The National Carbon Company sponsored the first regular entertainment program, "The Eveready Hour," as a vehicle for encouraging greater use of radios and thus a greater need for the batteries they manufactured.

By 1929, radios were in about 40% of U.S. homes. Advertisers modified their mnemonics to accommodate radio. Jingles became a prominent device for this purpose. Studies at the time reported that listeners were more prone to like advertising when it was presented in jingle form rather than merely spoken. The practice of using jingles is still prevalent today in radio advertising.

As the advertising industry grew, attempts were made by the industry to self-regulate. In the early 1900s, trade associations emerged to police advertising practice. Among these institutions are the Association of American Advertising Agencies (4As), the trade association for ad agencies, and the Association of National Advertisers (ANA), the trade association for manufacturers.

1930-1947: The Era of Credibility Development

The onset of the Great Depression affected advertising practice. To accommodate consumers' limited budget, advertisers began using many incentives. These included premiums, prizes, and two-for-one deals. As these practices became widely used, brand loyalty dropped. For example, between 1929 and 1934, Hellman's mayonnaise market share dropped 22 points and Listerine's market share declined 12%.

During the Depression, the consumer movement emerged and a vocal group of consumer advocates began to question advertising practices. In books such as *100 Million Guinea Pigs,* published in 1933, and *Eat, Drink and be Wary,* published in 1935, consumers were warned about the abuses of advertising, and advertisers were urged to use the vehicle as a means of conveying product information rather than deception. From these concerns, Consumers' Union emerged as an organization to affirm truth in advertising. In 1938, the Wheeler-Lea Amendment to the Federal Trade Commission Act was passed, giving the FTC the power to regulate unfair practices.

Advertisers responded to their critics by changing the nature of advertising copy. Rather than relying on slogans and jingles to ensure consumer recall of the advertiser's brand, the goal of ad copy became salesmanship in print. This concept was made operational by telling consumers why they should buy the advertised product. Albert Lasker, head of the large Lord and Thomas agency, and his copywriter, John Kennedy, were perhaps the foremost proponents of the reason - why copy approach. In advertising Schlitz beer, Lasker announced that Schlitz had greater purity because the bottles were steam cleaned. Though all brewers used this method, Lasker preempted competitors from using this attribute, lest consumers view them as "me-too" brands. As Lasker's and Kennedy's success grew, most copywriters adopted the reason-why approach.

Efforts were also made to build a personal relationship with consumers. This approach was helped by the fact that radio had coverage of over 80% of U.S. homes by 1938. Advertisers sponsored programs on which they advertised their products. Credibility for the advertising claims was enhanced by having the talent in the program serve as spokespeople for the advertised brand. Comedian Bob Hope was the spokesperson for Pepsodent, and crooner Bing Crosby endorsed Kraft products. The current practice of using celebrity spokespeople is derived from the use of endorsers in radio advertising.

Producers of soap operas used devices other than advertising to promote their brands. Starting in the early 1930s, soap operas commanded a faithful daily national audience of housewives who were estimated to control over 90% of household expenditures. Advertisers who produced the shows would use the program's characters and story lines to sell product. For example, in one of the popular early soaps, *Today's Children*, Pillsbury portrayed Mother Moran, the lead character, as a homemaker, expert cook, and endearing mother who frequently baked with Pillsbury products. Today's product placement is based on these strategies.

The Depression also increased the demands clients made on agencies to provide empirical support for the strategies they recommended and for the impact of the campaigns they developed. Research institutions emerged to address these needs. Syndicated services such as Nielsen conducted surveys of product and media consumption. This information was used to plan targeting efforts and to select media vehicles. Gallup and other organizations developed measures of sales for food and drug items and measures of advertising readership.

By the 1940s, advertising had emerged as an element in the marketing mix that management might use to enhance profits. The value of branding and advertising began to appear in firms' financial statements. Royal Baking Powder valued its mark at $8 million, Coca-Cola at $5 million and Baker's at $1 million. Much of the value of these marks was attributed to the sustained presentation of their benefits in advertising.

1948-1969: The Era of Television

After World War II, there was phenomenal growth in the ownership of televisions. Between 1946 and 1952, TV ownership grew from ten thousand to 16 million sets in the U.S. This substantially increased the audience for TV and the cost of sponsorship grew accordingly. In 1941, an hour of sponsorship on evening television cost about $120, whereas the cost for this placement was over $50,000 in 1952. Today the cost of a 30 second spot can be over $600,000 for placement in popular programs and the average production cost for a 30 second TV spot is $350,000. For special events (e.g., Superbowl) this price can be as high as $3000000 for a 30 second spot.

Early television advertising used many of the techniques that had proven to be effective on radio. Jingles and slogans that were popularized using radio were transferred to television. Frequently, the main use of the visual aspect of the medium was to provide a beauty shot of the product. Advertisers also sponsored programs in which program talent served as brand spokespeople in advertising messages.

As advertisers were learning how to utilize the visual aspect of the television medium, they were also changing their approach to designing persuasive messages in response to market conditions that prevailed after WW II. Twelve million Americans returned from the war with a more precise knowledge of what products they wished to buy as well as an increased ability to purchase those products. Manufacturers armed with improved technology and manufacturing capacity attempted to respond to consumer demand by offering brands that were differentiated from competitive offerings. In this context, Lasker's reason-why approach was modified to focus on reasons that differentiated the brand from its competitors on dimensions important to consumers.

Rosser Reeves of the Ted Bates agency was a leader in shaping this trend. He developed what he termed a unique selling proposition. Reeves' notion was to focus on a reason to buy a brand that set it apart from the competition. Along these lines, Bates developed the campaign "Rolaids spells relief." This simple, straightforward advertising worked well when firms had a point of difference and when people were interested in purchasing the category and the brand.

The advent of TV also prompted a change in the ad agency personnel doing creative work. The copywriter, who had responsibility for the copy presented in an ad, increasingly collaborated with an art director, who was responsible for visual development of the context in which the copy was presented. Many of the initial art directors had careers as designers in Europe before the outbreak of WW II, when they fled to the U.S. Modern creative departments include creative directors and art directors.

The emergence of TV changed the role of radio in the 1950s. Advertising on radio was given the task of ensuring brand name recognition. Radio advertising typically featured jingles that reinforced the brand name.

In the 1960s, the novelty of advertising diminished as the amount of TV advertising grew. As a result, creative executions that enhanced the audience's attentiveness to an advertiser's message were needed. Doyle Dane Bernbach emerged as a prominent agency in the 1960s by using humor to tell a story about the product in use. For example, in an ad for Alka Seltzer, a man was shown gulping down Alka Seltzer in anticipation of having to eat meals his wife was describing from a cookbook. Ogilvy & Mather attempted to attract attention by presenting substantial amounts of information in their ads with the idea that "the more you tell, the more you sell." Often the information presented included unusual visual devices to attract attention. For example, advertising for Hathaway featured a man wearing an eye patch, and advertising for Rolls Royce focused on the quietly ticking clock. Leo Burnett attempted to provide news by finding a consumer benefit that was substantial enough so that it could be represented by many attributes. Burnett promoted the Green Giant brand by using different packaging characteristics (fresh frozen, vacuum packed) to imply quality.

1970-1990: Era of Planning

As consumers became more educated and affluent, there was a growing emphasis on the development of products that catered to their individual tastes. The result was a huge proliferation of products. For example, today supermarkets often carry as many as 30,000 stock keeping units (SKU; the space taken at retail by a single product package), whereas a decade ago 20,000 SKUs were more typical and in the 1970s supermarkets typically had 12,000 SKUs. There was one Tide in the '70s; there were 10 different Tides by the early 90s. This product proliferation had an important implication for advertising. It required advertisers to support four of five campaigns rather than one or two. This practice, coupled with sharply increasing media rates, meant that many firms lost the ability to sustain advertising support.

To compensate for their relatively smaller budgets, advertisers sought ways to enhance the efficiency of their advertising expenditures. For this purpose, greater attention was devoted to the advertising function. Planning involves identifying the various groups that are potential prospects for a firm's products, selecting the targets that are particularly attractive prospects, and identifying a category where a brand can leverage its point of difference with the desired target. Thus, the planning era was characterized by a focus on segmentation, targeting and positioning (STP).

The creative strategy employed to make the plan operational reflects the various approaches that have been developed over the history of advertising practice. The choice of a specific approach is sensitive to the particular needs of the context at hand. Thus, when the situation is one where persuasion depends on brand name familiarity, a brand name repetition strategy that was popularized at the beginning of the 20th century is appropriate. Along these lines, in the context of aldermanic elections, candidate choice is based on name recognition and therefore repetition of the name is valuable. When a brand has leadership in a category where the brands are at parity, featuring a benefit that is common to rival brands can be made persuasive by outspending competition. Finally, when a brand has a unique benefit that is important to consumers, point of difference advertising is appropriate.

1990-2000: The Era of Value

In the last decade of the century, profound economic, political, and technological change has affected consumers' dispositions and firms' market responses. During the 1980s, Americans on average increased their workweek from 40 hours to 48 hours and reduced leisure time from 21 to 16 hours. These trends left consumers time famished. In addition, a severe economic downturn in the late 1980s made people more price sensitive than they had been since the early 1980s. The result was a change in how consumers viewed value. In the 1980s, brands were considered to have value if they offered extraordinary quality at a high price. By contrast, in the early 1990s, a parity product at a low price became criteria for ascertaining value in many product categories. Moreover, cost was assessed not just in terms of price, but also in terms of time. Products that fostered time efficiency were preferred, and ones that allowed the consumer to multi-task became popular. Time famine gave rise to greater emphasis on the product's psychic and hedonic benefits. This led to the value equation discussed in **Chapter 5**.

Consumers' focus on value reduced the attractiveness of branded products. Prices of branded products had increased substantially during the 1980s and were high in relation to private-label items. Moreover, in many categories, private-label brands had substantially improved their quality. The result was that in numerous categories, private-label products became substantial and sometimes leading brands. Even in a category such as analgesics where branded products have been preferred because people refuse to take risks when pain is involved, private label brands have the greatest volume share.

The trend toward product proliferation also worked in favor of the private-label brands. Faced with extreme time famine, consumers were unwilling to examine the 61 different cover sheets on the back of Always sanitary pad, or the 32 different forms of Crest, or the 30 variations of Head and Shoulders shampoo. Instead, they often based their purchase decision on price. In many categories, market share of major brands fell substantially.

The typical response to these events was to cut cost and compete with private-label items more closely on a price basis. This entailed finding ways to reduce the cost of goods, their distribution, and product management. Advertising expenditures continued to erode in favor of price promotions. The split in spending between advertising and consumer promotions, which had been 70:30 in favor of advertising in 1980, was 30:70 in favor of promotion by 1990. Clubs that featured low price and rotated the selection of the national brands they carried grew in popularity.

These strategies were successful in teaching consumers that products were at parity and that the choice decision should be based on price. Consumers got the message. Indeed, the focus on building the business rather than on building brands resulted in the share erosion of these brands. Maxwell House coffee lost about half its share when it focused its marketing support on consumer and trade price incentives. In addition, brand switching grew dramatically, and consumers' recall of advertising dropped. In short, the marketing strategies of the 1990s and consumers' reactions to them repeated the pattern described earlier for the 1930s.

The focus on low price put a squeeze on profits, which prompted vigorous efforts to reduce the cost of marketing efforts. Cost containment involved downsizing the organization and restructuring managers' activities. In many consumer package firms, for example, upper level management participates in cross-functional teams with the goal of containing costs. Middle level management is focused on category management, which entails managing the micro marketing efforts at retail. These organizational changes combined with the downsizing of organizations that characterized the early 1990s resulted in advertising planning often being left to the agency, consultants or to the retail buyer!

By the mid-1990s, when major cost containment programs were in place, marketers turned to rebuilding their brands. This entailed efforts to reduce consumer confusion about the essence of the brand by drastically cutting the number of brand offerings. Procter & Gamble reduced the varieties of Head and Shoulders from 30 to 15 and the cover sheets for Always from 61 to 13. Overall, P&G cut the total number of items they offered for sale by 30% over a five year period, during which time the percentage by which unit sales grew increased to 6%.

Efforts to build consumer brands have involved not only consolidating the number of brand flankers, but also the adoption of price stability programs so that focus would be on a brand's features rather than on its price. Consumer incentives were reduced and advertising spending was increased. Indeed, the 3% annual increase in ad budgets that were common in the late 1980s and early 1990s have been supplanted by annual budget increases that were on average between six and 11 percent in the 1990s.

In the late 1990s, increasing economic prosperity and consumer affluence prompted renewed focus on product quality. The result was significant growth in the sales of high end products. Gillette introduced the Mach 3, a blade that is priced at a 35% premium over their Sensor brand with good success. Hefty experienced a 45% sales increase with the introduction of their OneZip premium priced baggies. Kimberly-Clark had success with its premium diapers, in a category that grew to be 20% of the diaper business. This prompted others manufacturers to follow suit with a spate of high-end products. Oral B introduced the first $5 toothbrush in a category where products are typically priced at less than $3. Williams-Sonoma offered the Dualit, a $300+ hand assembled toaster. And, P&G introduced Physique Haircare for men at a price point of $7, which was about twice the average price charged in the category at the time.

Consumers' preference for high-end brands is reminiscent of consumer response during the last wave of consumer affluence in the mid-1980s. The difference is that in the 1980s high-end consumption was conspicuous and in high priced categories such as watches and cars. The more recent high-end purchases were for functional items.

The 2000's: Adding Value Through Customer Insight

Advertising expenditures grew dramatically in 1999 and 2000 fueled by initial efforts at marketing Internet companies. With the downturn in economic conditions, there was a significant decline in ad spending starting in 2002. In reaction, communication institutions have sought to increase the value they add in enhancing communication effects. Print media, which have been hard hit by the cuts in ad spending, have sought to add value by providing agencies and their clients with more detailed information not only about the users of various media, but more generally about the activities, interests, and opinions of segments that are of interest to advertisers. Agencies have attempted to add value to their clients by developing comprehensive communication programs rather than ones based on mass media vehicles. Thus, agencies seek to offer integrated campaigns utilizing both traditional media forms, such as television, and evolving media forms, such as the Internet. Manufacturers, and particularly consumer package good firms, have attempted to add value by using their knowledge of customers to help redesign retail space so as to communicate brand positions more effectively in-store. Thus, the communication channel that was once a loose coalition of entities is now better characterized as a series of partnerships developed with the goal of adding value through the distribution of knowledge about the customer.

With the emergence of the Internet there has been realignment in the use of media for advertising. Newspapers, which depend on revenues from want ads, have been hard hit by online services that accomplish the same goal at a lower price such as Craigslist. Magazines have suffered substantial declines in audience, which has prompted advertisers to develop their own custom magazines. Lexus, for example, has a magazine that includes news about its brands that it sends to current owners as well as individuals in upscale zip codes. Firms have made increasing use of the Internet, both in terms of using search engines such as Google, to direct customers to their web sites, and in developing web pages that inform and entertain consumers. Greater focus now centers on trying to reach consumers when they are decisional about the category using mobile advertising, outdoor advertising, and event sponsorship.

As the economic downturn became more severe, advertising has focused more on product value. This has resulted in brands engaging in more comparative advertising to highlight the value offered. For example, Progresso and Campbell soups compare the nutritional value of their brands against each other. Other brands have tied their equity to the challenging economic times. Along these lines, Allstate advertising emphasizes that the safety it provides is even more important under current economic conditions. And luxury brands such as DeBeers diamonds advertises the importance of purchasing less, but purchasing objects that will have enduring value—such as diamonds.